RAISING YOUR CHILD,
NOT YOUR VOICE

RAISING YOUR CHILD, NOT YOUR VOICE

Dr. Duane Cuthbertson

While this book is intended for the reader's personal enjoyment and profit, it is also intended for group study. A Leader's Guide with Victor Multiuse Transparency Masters is available from your local bookstore or from the publisher.

VICTOR BOOKS™
A DIVISION OF SCRIPTURE PRESS PUBLICATIONS INC.
USA CANADA ENGLAND
94291

The chart on page 105 is from *Child Psychology: A Developmental Perspective* by William Meyer and Jerome Dusek. Copyright © 1979 by D.C. Heath and Company. Reprinted by permission of the publisher.

Material drawn from *Temperament and Behavioral Disorders in Children* by Alexander Thomas, Stella Chess, and Herbert G. Birch, copyright © 1968 by New York University, is used by permission of New York University Press.

Most Scripture quotations are from the *King James Version* of the Bible. Other quotations are from the *The Living Bible*, ©1971, Tyndale House Publishers, Wheaton, IL 60189. Used by permission.

Recommended Dewey Decimal Classification: 301.42

Suggested Subject Heading: MARRIAGE AND FAMILY

Library of Congress Catalog Card Number: 86-60870
ISBN: 0-89693-342-3

Contents

Preface

Either we are raising our children, or our children are raising us. A lot of us have had the latter experience. When it comes to child rearing, we just don't know what we're doing. As a matter of fact, if we were asked where we learned to become parents, many of us would have to acknowledge our ignorance. Or we would have to admit that we subconsciously operate on the premise that our parents did it right—and we do it *their* way.

The parent who raises his voice instead of his child is saying, "I don't understand how to be a parent." We can all sympathize. But Proverbs 16:32 states, "He that is slow to anger is better than the mighty, and he that ruleth his spirit than he that taketh a city." The last time you got angry at your child, were you "slow to anger"? Did you say, "In five minutes I am going to be upset; in ten minutes I am going to become a raving maniac"? No? I think most of us just react and let our emotions lead us.

The challenge of the Proverbs passage is to rule our spirits. I hope this book will help you do just that—by helping you to better understand yourself *and* your child. It is also my prayer that as you are introduced to the concept of Assertive Scriptural Parenting, you will gain a deeper certainty of God's purposes in your life.

1

We're All in This Together

Being a parent is *not* as simple as ABC. That's probably why you're reading this book. The purpose of these pages is to develop a biblical view of child rearing, using the Bible as the authority. Recent psychological studies will be used too. The goal is to help you hone your parenting skills, gain a biblical perspective on what constitutes failure and success in child rearing, understand the process of "will modification," and recognize the "bent" of each of your children.

If this sounds like a lot, don't worry. I'm a parent too. We're all in this together. So let's take it a step at a time.

Parenting: Success and Failure
If you have five children in full-time Christian work, you might conclude, "Hey, I did it! You other parents want to know about child rearing? Come to me. After all, look at my kids." But the results may be due exclusively to the mercy and sovereignty of God. Conversely,

you may have done everything possible to raise a child in the "nurture and admonition of the Lord" (Eph. 6:4)—and that child could be a "zero" spiritually. You may be filled with guilt and assume the responsibility of failure. Either way, the idea of success and failure in parenting can be confusing as well as intimidating.

I vividly remember being called to the office of a pastor friend. He had two sons, neither of whom was a Christian. One was a homosexual. As an outsider I had thought that the pastor and his wife must have "blown it" somewhere. But as the pastor began that day to share his grief concerning his boys, I started to see how little I knew of the situation. I was overwhelmed as the man began to cry uncontrollably, burying his head on my shoulder and sobbing. Who was to blame for this family tragedy? I wondered. Was it the devil? Was it God? Was it the kids themselves? That pastor's dilemma, in part, stimulated the writing of this book.

A great heart cry echoes from 2 Samuel 18:33. After the death of his son Absalom, David laments, "O my son Absalom! My son, my son Absalom!" The grief and pain that pour from the broken hearts of broken parents can be stunning.

Children can "go wrong" regardless of a parent's education or intent. There is the psychology professor with four children, all of whom have deep emotional problems. There is the pastor whose daughter has rejected his beliefs and rejected him as well. You've seen other examples in your church and neighborhood.

Why does this happen? Partly because parents can work only from what they know—which is often limited to their own parents' example. It also happens because most of us can deal much more objectively with others' problems than with our own. Many who should "know better" become very subjective in raising their own children.

There is also the problem of expectations. "My child *will* go to college, if it kills me," says one parent. Even if it doesn't kill, the emotional strain such a parent places on himself can be overpowering—as can the strain on the child.

Some of us are like the man who long ago bought a thoroughbred horse, convinced he had purchased wealth and fame. After all, didn't this horse have the best of blood lines? Hadn't the sire won the Kentucky Derby? But after twelve races in which the horse finished last, the owner began to wonder. Finally, before the thirteenth race, he lifted the horse's ear and said, "This is it for you. Either you win this race, or you are going to be pulling a milk wagon in the morning.

The race began. It was a beautiful start, with the horse lunging to the front. But at the half pole, he began his familiar fade. In desperation, the jockey went to the whip. As he beat on the side of the horse, the horse suddenly turned to him, looked him straight in the eye, and said, "Please, go easy on that whip. I have to get up at 4:30 in the morning to deliver milk!"

Like the owner of that horse, many of us establish goals for our children and drive them hard. After all, didn't they come from good blood lines (us)? But like that horse, our children just might not have it in them.

The raising of children can place untold stress on both child and parent. For that reason we must learn and apply biblical principles to this process. If raising children is our "plight and joy," we must approach it "armed and ready."

How Children Develop

Most people would probably agree that a child's temperament and environment determine much of his development. But as Christians, we believe it all begins with a more important factor: God's sovereignty. Psalm 139:13-16 indicates that God weaved that child according to His own design while the child was being carried in the womb. Even at that fragile state of growth, the child's days were "numbered."

God is in charge. "The king's heart is in the hand of the Lord, as the rivers of water: He turneth it whithersoever He will" (Prov. 21:1). "By Me kings reign and princes decree justice. By Me princes rule, and nobles, even all the judges of the earth" (Prov. 8:15-16). God is not surprised at anything, as 2 Timothy 1:9 implies: God, "who hath saved us and called us with an holy calling, not according to our works, but according to His own purpose and grace, which was given us in Christ Jesus Before the world began."

Before the world began, God saw Nicky Cruz, who had spiritualists for parents in Puerto Rico; who was dropped on the streets of New York City at thirteen; who, through a "wave of circumstances" understood only by God, eventually became a Christian, attended Bible school, and began to serve as an evangelist. I believe God saw Nicky Cruz doing all that, even when Nicky had a knife to someone's throat on the streets of New York City. God saw it before the foundation of the world.

And what about the Apostle Paul? Or Peter? We know these men did not come from Christian homes either. I don't understand God's selection process, but I do know they were called and chosen—before the world began.

God is also sovereign in choosing our children's genetic characteristics. I have no control over my child's temperament, for example. I have to take what God sends me. There are so many variations possible in intelligence, personality, motor skills, and physical appearance. My wife, for instance had a great-grandmother who was 4'10" tall. I have a cousin who is some 7'4" tall, weighs 440 pounds and used to work as a constable in North Carolina. When I asked him what he did to break up a fight, he said, "I just show up." That height difference is quite a variable.

Sure, it would be fine if God had given us a boy, 6'6", compliant, brilliant, spiritual, personable, and athletic—or the female counterpart. But He didn't. He gave us what He wanted us to have. He has something different for each of us: "But now hath God set the members every one of them in the body, as it hath pleased Him" (1 Cor. 12:18).

The environmental factor, on the other hand, is the only one we can control to some degree. That in itself can be an exhausting task.

As parents we make decisions daily as to how much our children can be "stretched." We decide how much stress we will place on them. We decide, consciously or not, whether their security needs will be met.

These decisions can make indelible impressions on our children. That was the case with a girl I first met in a hospital's intensive care unit. She and her father had been arguing in their front yard. He had tackled her, knocked her to the ground, and held her there with his knees over her arms. He struck her in the face again and again with his fists. Even after he knocked her out, he kept hitting. Finally neighbors literally dragged him off her. The girl almost died of her injuries. During her recovery I counseled her.

About ten years later it was my privilege to counsel this girl and her fiancé in preparation for their marriage. As the two of them met with me, I asked her this simple question: "What about your father?" Immediately she broke into tears. She had not forgotten, and she never will.

Not all parenting decisions are as extreme or lasting in their effects, of course. But many of them can "bend" our children for better or worse.

Train Up a Child

The core of this book is Proverbs 22:6: "Train up a child in the way he should go, and when he is old, he will not depart from it." Charles Swindoll, in his book *You and Your Child,* states, "Some contemporary religious interpretations would paraphrase the verse: 'Be sure your child is in Sunday School and church regularly. Cement into his mind a few memorized verses from the Bible plus some hymns and prayers. Send him to Christian camps during the summers of his formative years, and certainly, if at all possible, place the child in a Christian school, so he can be educated by people whose teaching is based on the Bible. Because, after all, someday he will sow wild oats. For sure, he will have his fling. But when he gets old enough to get over his fling, he will come back to God.'"[1] But form and structure are not enough to "train up" a child. Some of our worst "products" were regular churchgoers. They were *made* to attend church.

A girl I'll call Kathy was made to attend church. Kathy used to sit in the back of the church with a radio in her purse, unknown to the rest of the congregation. Thus she sat during worship service, with the cord running up her dress to the plug in her ear; she was listening to the local rock station.

Another girl, Barbara, was made to go to church; then she was pressed to attend a Christian college. When she went off to that school it was "national liberation day" for her. During the next three months she experienced most everything that was morally and socially bad. In her mind, she had to make up for lost time. She was asked to leave the school.

So it is with many children raised in a context that is *religious,* but not *correct.* They think, *I don't want to become too religious. I might miss something.*

In these pages we will explore Proverbs 22:6 from both biblical and psychological standpoints. This verse in the familiar *King James Version* reads, "Train up a child in the way he should go, and when he is old he will not depart from it." A loose paraphrase of the passage, consistent with the original writings, might be, "Modify the will of the child, the way he is bent, and when he gets to be a teenager, that pattern will stay with him." Note that the "will modification," or mind-changing, process has to be consistent with the "bent," or temperament, of the child. The environment and the temperament must work together. A sensitive child in a hostile environment could be devastated; a defiant child might not make it in a home with two overly compliant parents.

Sound complicated? You won't need a degree in psychology to use will modification and recognize the bent of your child. The terms may sound fancy, but the ideas are down-to-earth—which reminds me of a story:

Three dogs met on the street one day. Two of them were pedigreed females; one was a male mutt.

The mutt looked at the "young ladies" and inquired, "What are your names?"

With her nose high in the air, one replied, "My name is Fifi; that is spelled F-I-F-I."

He turned to "lady" number two and asked, "And your name?"

In an equally snobbish way she said, "Mimi; that's spelled M-I-M-I."

"Nice to meet you," said the mutt, not to be outdone. "My name is Fido. That's spelled, P-H-Y-D-E-A-U-X."

This book is for all the "Fidos" in the world. In reality we are all the same—struggling and human. As for me, what I have learned about parenting I have learned in self-defense.

2

New Kids, Old Nature

My wife had fixed an excellent chicken casserole for dinner. But Tami, our second little girl, decided she was not going to eat. She had eaten this dish many times before, but had made up her mind not to do so that night.

"Tami, are you feeling all right?" I asked.

"Yes," she said.

"You're not sick?" I asked.

"No."

"Tami, please understand that you are expected to eat your dinner," I said. "Is that clear?"

"Yes."

Still she would not eat the casserole. So I tried another approach.

"Tami, you don't want to see your mother cry, do you? After all, she has worked hours on this casserole."

That didn't seem to affect her either. I became desperate.

"Tami, if you don't eat your supper, your father will spank you. Is that clear?" I said.

"Yes."

"Are you going to eat it?"

"No."

So I spanked her. Still she would not eat the casserole. When I threatened to spank her again, I got a look from my wife that seemed to say, "Are you sure you know what you're doing?" The expression on my face was meant to assure her that I was doing the best I could.

Finally I looked at Tami and said, "Tami, open your mouth." She opened her mouth. "Tami, keep your mouth open," I said. I proceeded to pick out the best piece of chicken casserole I could find and put it right on her tongue.

"Tami, close your mouth," I said. She closed her mouth. "Tami, chew the food." She chewed the food. "Tami, swallow the food." She swallowed the food. I looked at her and said, "Tami, that wasn't bad, was it?"

She shook her head. Then she sat down to eat the rest of her supper.

I must confess that this approach was at best a calculated risk. But it worked.

What was at stake that night? Chicken casserole? No. The issue was not whether my daughter ate her food. The issue was that at the ripe old age of four, she had decided to bring her will to bear; suddenly we had a father-versus-daughter confrontation of wills.

It is the *will* of the child that becomes his or her "rudder" in life. Parents strive to conform the wills of their children to their own, explicitly or otherwise. And the fact is that "will modification"—changing the child's tendency to follow the old nature—is absolutely imperative. But it isn't easy. This chapter will analyze the difficulties in this process.

Kids and Wild Horses

Remember our key verse: "Train up a child in the way he should go and when he is old, he will not depart from it" (Prov. 22:6). Our paraphrase of the verse is, "Modify the will of the child, the way he is bent, and when he gets to be a teenager, the pattern will stay with him." When applied, this little verse is the backbone of Christian education.

The words "train up" (*chanuk* in Hebrew) imply two ideas: *the necessity of modifying the will,* and *the fact that the child learns by example.* The Hebrew word carries the meaning of "needing to be brought into submission" and "imitation or discipline." Note the parental responsibility in both of these concepts.

Explaining "train up" in his book, *You and Your Child,* Charles Swindoll writes:

> The original root word is the term for "the palate, the roof of the mouth, the gums." In verb form, it is the term used for breaking and bringing into submission a wild horse by a rope in the mouth. The term was also used in the days of Solomon to describe the action of a midwife who, soon after helping to deliver a child, would dip her finger into the juice of chewed or crushed dates, reach into the mouth of the infant, and massage the gums and the palate within the mouth so as to create a sensation of sucking, a sense of taste. The juice was also believed to be a cleaning agent in the newborn's mouth. Then she would place the child in the mother's arms to begin feeding from the mother's breast. So . . . "train up" is used to describe the "developing of a thirst."[2]

We can all understand the midwife analogy. But breaking a wild horse? How is it possible for a dear, cuddly, warm, loving infant to be like a wild stallion?

Sherri was our first of five children. She was an absolutely gorgeous baby. Within minutes after her birth the nurses had placed a ribbon in her beautiful red hair. When I first saw her, I was afraid to touch her; she looked like a china doll. But when we took her home, that all changed. She had developed a mild colicky condition, and because of the pain, cried *constantly*. My wife and I would take turns through the night walking the floor with her. I must admit that at about 4 A.M. I was tempted to lower the pat on her back.

No parent needs to be reminded that even the sweet, cuddly, loving child has a sin nature. Even we adults might, on *rare* occasions, see it in ourselves.

For me, the simplest description of our sin nature is found in David's outcry: "Have mercy upon me, O God, according to Thy loving-kindness: according unto the multitude of Thy tender mercies blot out my *transgressions*. Wash me thoroughly from mine *iniquity*, and cleanse me from my *sin*" (Ps. 51:1-2, italics added). David was begging forgiveness from God for his sin with Bathsheba. In the depth of his contrition, David delved into three phases of the sin nature: (1)*transgression* (Hebrew, *pasha*), which means "we are in a state of rebellion and revolt"; (2) *iniquity (avown),* "bent away from God"; and (3) *sin (cheta),* "to miss the mark."

Of the three parts of our sin nature, one can be blotted out. It is our rebellion, our transgressions. The word for "blot out" is the Hebrew word *machah,* which means "to abolish, destroy, eradicate." Child or adult, I don't *have* to slam the door or poke someone in the eye. That part of me can be eradicated.

What does this mean for you as a parent? *That your child's will can be modified.*

I must emphasize strongly that children are born with an old, sinful nature. The bent of a child is naturally toward rebellion, away from God, toward unrighteousness. Unless deliberate steps are taken to modify that child's will, the results could be disastrous.

Discipline and the Will
Will modification requires disciplining the child. Verses like 1 Corinthians 6:19-20; 9:27 clearly state that the goal of proper discipline is "subjection of the body." Any good athlete will tell you that in order for the body to be in subjection, there must be discipline.

Throughout high school and college I was involved in athletics. I was a jumper; I enjoyed the high jump, long jump, and pole vault. One year I was fortunate enough to be captain of the team, and with that came a large dose of adolescent pride. Thus at one track meet I told our coach I would like to run the mile. I had not *trained* for the mile; I had trained to be a jumper. But we were up against a weak team, so the coach granted my request. The race started. For the first of four laps I was easily ahead and held that position at the half-mile point. But during the third lap I began to weaken, and two people passed me. By the fourth lap I was a disaster. My body was exhausted, and I remember fighting off another fellow as we vied for last place. I simply had not disciplined my body to be a miler.

So it is with our youngsters. Through discipline their hearts must be changed. "Foolishness is bound in the heart of a child; but the rod of correction shall drive it far from him" (Prov. 22:15). We must constantly remind ourselves that "the heart is deceitful . . . and desperately wicked: who can know it?" (Jer. 17:9)

Only wisdom can recognize foolishness. It is godly wisdom that discerns that the core of foolish behavior is not merely a youth's environment or low I.Q.; it is the intrinsic *nature* of that child. If the fear of God is the principle of wisdom, the principle of foolishness is rebellion—and only discipline can drive it out.

At least two characteristics of foolishness are described in the Book of Proverbs: (1) it is displayed through words (17:28); and (2) it is shown *through the absence of a teachable heart* (10:8; 12:15; 15:5). Room must be made in the child's heart before wisdom can be planted and take root.

When foolishness or rebellion manifests itself, it must be dealt with or it will grow. The goal is to separate the child from his foolishness, and the stick of discipline is the pruning instrument that works. The rod drives foolishness away from the child.

Spare the Rod?

Discipline is the means by which the will is modified. In Ephesians 6:4 the following command is given: "Ye fathers, provoke not your children to wrath: but bring them up in the nurture and admonition of the Lord." The word translated "nurture" is the Greek word *paideia,* which means "to give instruction, to chasten." The word is translated "chastening" three times in Hebrews 12:5, 7, and 11, and the verb form of the word is translated "chastise" in Luke 23:16 and 22, where Pilate said about Jesus, "I will therefore chastise Him."

God puts chastening before instruction. He knows that the will must be prepared before the child will listen to teaching. This is the most crucial part of child rearing. We don't *beat* our children or take out our own frustrations and unresolved problems on them; but we don't refuse to spank them, thinking that physical punishment is "barbaric." The purpose of corporal punishment is to modify the will so that the child can learn discipline; if that will is not bent, the child could be fighting with a spouse later in life or arguing constantly with coworkers. The Bible makes it clear that verbal discipline and instruction of children are sometimes not enough:

He that spareth his rod hateth his son; but he *that loveth* him chasteneth him betimes (Prov. 13:24).

Chasten thy son while there is hope, and let not thy soul spare for his crying (19:18).

Foolishness is bound in the heart of a child; but the rod of correction shall drive it far from him (22:15).

Withhold not correction from the child . . . thou shalt beat him with the rod, and shalt deliver his soul from hell (23:13-14).

The rod and reproof give wisdom; but a child left to himself bringeth his mother to shame (29:15).

It is vital, however, that you never, *never,* lose touch with the *pur-pose* of discipline. Your goal is to lovingly modify the child's will, not to vent your anger. It is done because of the child's old nature, because the child is in rebellion, is bent away from God, and has missed the mark.

Overdiscipline is counterproductive. I believe a youngster knows inherently—though perhaps subconsciously—that he has done wrong and what is deserved as punishment. You don't take up a belt and put welts across his or her back for sneaking a cookie from the jar. Overdiscipline does not *modify* the will; it *reinforces* the will. The overdisciplined child is ready to fight back, and will look for any means available to hurt you. Many times "religion" becomes his battleground.

The will must always be modified *in love and self-control.* Then, in time, the child will learn to put his body—his old nature—in subjection to the will of God.

3

Eight Steps to a Changed Heart

As a parent, you can work to modify your child's will during his or her infancy. Failing that, you can try again during childhood and the teenage years. But if that doesn't work, it's up to God. Only He can modify the will of an adult.

To understand how will modification works, we need to examine how God modifies an adult's will. His example is in some ways a pattern for the steps we must take with our children.

The fourth chapter of the Book of James provides a step-by-step guide to how God changes the will. These seventeen verses move in a progression, I believe, reaching the climactic conclusion that *God wants us to give our wills back to Him.* We should learn, grasp, and memorize these steps. They reveal not only how God changes our hearts but also the dynamics employed in modification of our children's wills.

✿ Step One: Recognize

First of all, we must *recognize the inadequacy of the human will:*

> From whence come wars and fightings among you? Come they not hence, even of your lusts that war in your members? Ye lust and have not; ye kill and desire to have, and cannot obtain: ye fight and war, yet ye have not, because ye ask not. Ye ask, and receive not, because ye ask amiss, that ye may consume it upon your lusts. Ye adulterers and adulteresses, know ye not that the friendship of the world is enmity with God? Whosoever therefore will be a friend of the world is the enemy of God. Do ye think that the Scripture saith in vain, "The spirit that dwelleth in us lusteth to envy"? (James 4:1-5)

The word *members* refers to our different parts as persons. We are told in 1 Thessalonians 5:23, "And the very God of peace sanctify you wholly, and I pray God your whole *spirit* and *soul* and *body* be preserved blameless unto the coming of our Lord Jesus Christ" (italics added). Notice these three basic members, also mentioned in Genesis 2:7 and Hebrews 4:12. Emotions, intellect, memory, and the will are also among our members. It is the *will* that creates wars and fightings among our members. It is the will that strikes back. It is the will that activates anger, bitterness, and hate. "Ye lust . . . ye kill and desire to have, and cannot obtain." That describes the human will's tendencies in a nutshell.

"Who does he think he is, pushing me around?" we say. "I'm not going to let my children talk to me that way." That's the human will talking.

The world says, "Become strong-willed." God says, "Give up; let Me fight for you." Exodus 14:14: "The Lord shall fight for you, and ye shall hold your peace."

When I was little, my mother used to spank me (deservedly so, I'm sure). Later she would come up to me to kiss me and make up.

My response was, "Get away from me!" My hands would shoot over my face. "I don't want you to kiss me!" In other words, *You've hurt me; so I will hurt you.* I was being willful.

The human will, thanks to the old nature, is simply not up to the task of raising children or being raised. A will-to-will confrontation is not the answer in raising our children. We need to have our hearts changed.

Step Two: Understand

Second, we must *understand humility.* James 4:6, 10: "But He giveth more grace. Wherefore He saith, 'God resisteth the proud but giveth grace unto the humble.' . . . Humble yourselves in the sight of the Lord, and He shall lift you up."

Some of us understand humility more easily than others do. People who need help with their marriages, for example, are strong-willed individuals. But none of us can skip this step toward will modification.

Understanding and practicing humility is the turning point of will modification. Having grasped who we are in relationship to God, we can develop the proper attitude. That's not easy in our humanistic society, which says that if you are a good speaker, outstanding athlete, successful business person, or honor student, you have earned the right to be proud, even haughty. Still the Apostle Paul wrote, "But what things were gain to me, those I counted loss for Christ" (Phil. 3:7).

God wants us to become His students, just as we want our children to learn from us. For this to happen, our pride must be broken and replaced by humility; our children must sense our dependence on the Lord. Crises and struggles must lead to contrition. God deserves nothing less.

Step Three: Submit

Third, we must *submit to God.* James 4:7: "Submit yourselves therefore to God. Resist the devil, and he will flee from you."

The words *resist* and *submit* definitely speak to our wills. If I ask you to do something, you have two options: you can say yes and submit to my will, or say no and resist.

This is true at home too. Confrontations in most homes are built around arguments—making the bed, taking out the garbage, raking the leaves, etc. Do you find yourself gladly submitting? Or do you find yourself resisting, arguing, and bickering?

We resist Satan by recognizing temptation before it conceives and then refusing to yield to it. It is the temptation that leads to lust, sin, and death (James 1:13-15). You can choose not to heed God's will, but never forget Galatians 6:7: "Be not deceived, God is not mocked; for whatsoever a man soweth, that shall he also reap." Even as I was writing these words, a girl told me she was rejecting God and giving herself to the occult, drugs, sex, and alcohol. She had made her choice.

God could easily *take* our wills, but He lets us *give* them to Him—if we choose. He wants us to want Him. He wants us to desire righteousness and holiness. He allows us the choice.

What does this mean for child rearing? We can attempt to force our wills on our children and end up with either clones or rebels. Or we can model God's love, submit to Him, and watch our children subconsciously submit their wills to us so that they can grow. It is a joy to have children who are "just like us"—when we have something good to imitate.

Step Four: Be Clean

Fourth, we must *be clean.* James 4:8: "Draw nigh to God and He will draw nigh to you. Cleanse your hands, ye sinners, and purify your hearts, ye double-minded." God wants us to be clean—and that is an act of the will too.

Our society, in the name of freedom, thrives on filth. Satan has taken so much that God meant to be good and made it dirty. As we give ourselves to these activities, we can become soiled and spotted.

Recently I counseled a high school girl at a church retreat. She went to church, appeared to live by all the rules, was the secretary of the church youth group, and at that retreat played the piano. But she said, "Duane, I want to tell you what I am *really* like and what I am *really* doing." She told me that about every other weekend she would go to the home of her sister, who was not a Christian. From Friday night to Sunday afternoon this "fine Christian girl" would live like the devil with her sister. Then she would return home on Sunday, telling her mother how she and her sister "shared spiritual truths."

Now, with tears flowing down her cheeks, she said, "What a phony I've been. Will God ever forgive me?"

Many of us, like that girl, find it hard to be clean vessels for God's spirit. But our children need and desire clean models.

Step Five: Be Broken

Next, we must *be broken.* "Be afflicted and mourn and weep: let your laughter be turned into mourning and your joy to heaviness" (James 4:9). Most of us have to go through a breaking process before the Lord can use us.

I spent part of my growing-up years on the streets of Detroit. There it was a matter of will against will—of who was the strongest, fought the hardest, or was the most aggressive. During that time I did not know what tears were. I did not know what it meant to be so concerned about someone else that I could cry; I considered crying a sign of weakness. But God was right and I was wrong. Before He could use me, God had to take me through a breaking process.

Perhaps you've had a similar experience. Your marriage went through rough waters before it began to stabilize, or you know heartache concerning your children.

For me, one of the most sobering "breaking points" in my life came as I drove home from college. After a full day of activity, I received an emergency phone call and left to make the 200-mile drive to Detroit. After driving most of the night I fell asleep at the wheel—and rolled the car down a hill. The car was completely demolished; the windows were shattered and the roof was pressed against the steering wheel. But by the grace of God, the only injury to me was a small cut on my nose.

God had a purpose in that experience. As the car was rolling over and over I was convinced I was going to die. But it was part of God's design to help me see how strong-willed I was. I had to learn the hard way.

As parents, we need to use disciplinary times as learning experiences for our children—to bring good out of "bad." This is no new concept; we often spank our children on the premise that "this is for your own good."

"Johnny," we say, "you were spanked because you were playing in the street. Don't you realize that those cars could kill you?"

We do that not only to stop Johnny from playing in the street, but also because we want him to look to us for authority in other areas as well.

So does our Heavenly Father when He disciplines us.

Step Six: A New View

Next, we must *view people differently.* When we are truly broken, when our wills begin to change, we will see people in a much different light.

"Speak not evil one of another; he that speaketh evil of his brother and judgeth his brother speaketh evil of the Law and judgeth the Law" (James 4:11).

The will seems directly connected to the tongue. If you go through a breaking process, you begin to see—and speak of—your spouse, your children, and others from a much different perspective. You will find that walls built over the years are beginning to crumble. You will find that you are not trying to tear people down or trying to find people to reinforce your view of how "terrible" your spouse is. Instead you will be moving toward a deeper, more meaningful relationship with others.

One of my counseling sessions illustrated this. It involved a strained father-son relationship. The father was resistant from the beginning, sitting with a defiant look on his face. He made it clear that he wanted no part of the counseling process. His son had quit school, was using drugs heavily, and was about to ruin his life—but the father seemed to feel no sense of responsibility.

I talked to the parents and had three sessions with the son. I found that the father and son rarely talked. The problem had come to a head after the father wanted the son to paint the garage and the son resisted for weeks. One day when his father was away, the son decided to surprise his dad and paint the garage. The father returned home while the son was still painting—and began to criticize the young man's work. The son picked up the paint can, threw it at his father, jumped on his motorcycle, and left for five days.

The father, of course, was irate. He did not realize that in part *he* had caused that paint to be thrown at him.

I found the boy and encouraged him to return home. Then I met with the parents. After an hour of counseling, I told the father, "In a few minutes your son is going to walk into this house. I encourage you to go up to him, put your hands on his shoulders, and say, 'Son, I'm sorry. I have made many mistakes. Will you please forgive me? I want to be a better father.'" This was totally out of character for that strong-willed, belligerent man who had raised a strong-willed, belligerent son.

The son came shuffling in. The father walked over to him, put his hands on his shoulders, and said, "Son, I'm sorry. I have been a poor father. Will you ever forgive me?" The son looked at his father for a moment, then broke into tears. His father wept, his mother began crying, and the barriers began to fall. It had taken some seventeen years for the father and son to become acquainted. They had finally found one of the greatest gifts in life—one another.

God wants to change our relationships, and one evidence of such a change is our new view of others. The way we speak of and to each other shows what's in our hearts. If you want to discover the state of your child's heart, listen to the way he or she speaks.

✿ Step Seven: Release Your Rights

Next we need to *give God all rights to our lives.* James 4:13-14: "Go to now, ye that say, 'Today or tomorrow we will go into such a city and continue there a year, and buy and sell, and get gain': Whereas ye know not what shall be on the morrow. For what is your life? It is even a vapour that appeareth for a little time, and then vanisheth away."

God wants you to give up total rights to your material, psychological, or spiritual possessions. God wants you to give Him complete ownership of everything that is yours. That means you do not own anything—not a suit of clothes, not a car. God owns it all. This involves an exercise of your will.

Years ago I was a director for a Youth for Christ chapter. During the first year of involvement with Youth for Christ, my total salary was $250. The following year my total salary jumped to $1,000. One Christmastime my wife and I sat down with our bills and found that our total indebtedness came to $1,000. Our little boy was two years old, and we were convinced that the hospital was going to come get him for back payment! God has asked us to give up our "rights" to financial security and a prosperous style of living. But He also was faithful to provide for us. The night after we had added up our debts a friend handed me an envelope. He said, "Duane, my wife and I have prayerfully had you on our minds. We feel that God would have us give you this gift. This is not to go back into Youth for Christ. This is not to be part of your salary. It is a gift from my wife and me to you." He told me to take the envelope home and open it with my wife. When we opened the envelope—thinking optimistically that it might be a check for $50 or $100—we were stunned to find a check for $1,000.

The Bible says that God owns the cattle on a thousand hills and that He will do exceeding abundantly above all we could ask or think. Because God owns it all, we have nothing that He hasn't loaned to us. Giving up our rights to the things we think we own leads to rich blessing, not impoverishment. That was my wife's and my experience that Christmas.

God wants that house, that spouse—everything you claim as your own. When you recognize His ownership, you have a very different outlook on your home and family. Your will is modified further.

Our children see these patterns in our lives. They can become strong-willed if we are, with no concept of what it means to be humble, clean, broken, or submissive. Or, if we give up our rights to God, they can see our example and say, in effect, "Dad, Mom, I want to be like you." It's one thing for us to expect our children to "do as they are told." It's entirely another for them to *want* to do as they are told.

Can we be so presumptuous that we demand our children's wills without giving ours to God?

Step 8: Trade Wills

The final phase: Our wills *must be dissolved in His will.* "For you ought to say, 'If the Lord wills, we shall live to do this or that'" (James 4:15).

"If the Lord wills," we often say, and, "Lord willing." I used to think only superspiritual people said, "Lord willing." But all of us should use the phrases. We *are* here only by the grace of God.

Many turn this around and say, "If it be the Lord's will, I will go to Africa." Or, "If it be the Lord's will, I will change my life."

God really wants us to say, "Not my will, but Thine be done." He wants you to take your hands off your life and let Him run it for you.

Understanding, humility, submission, breaking ... all of these must happen before we can take our hands off our lives. God will not be satisfied until He gets holiness and righteousness from us, but He wants us to *want* it. That is why, step by step, He creates those circumstances necessary for the will modification process to happen in us.

Many of us blunder and stumble through life, wondering why crises happen to us. Paul in Romans 5:3 exhorts us to "glory in tribulations." I used to think, *Come on, you must be kidding!* But God uses those circumstances to change us. When we have given Him our wills, we can have confidence that, whether we understand it or not, He can run our lives better than we can.

To God, we will always be children. With the children He has entrusted to us, we can follow His example in the discipline, growth, and will modification of our children.

4

Definition of Discipline

The goal of discipline is to modify a child's will. The problem is his old nature. But what is the nature of discipline itself? Before we examine methods of will modification, we need a definition and philosophy of discipline.

Here is my definition: *Discipline is the means by which a goal is reached.*   ↳we modify a child's will.

Goal-Oriented Discipline
I cannot lose weight unless I discipline myself. I cannot get a college degree unless I discipline myself. Any individual struggle or personal aspiration demands discipline before it can be achieved.   ✗

The same is true in child rearing. Every act of discipline *should* ✗ *be goal-oriented.* We have our children say "Thank you" and "You're welcome," for example, *because* we want them to have

Example

good manners. We reprimand them when they play near the street *because* we want to keep them from getting hurt.

I've already used the illustration of my daughter Tami and her refusal to eat dinner. Did I see the goal during the discipline? I hope so. If your child has walked across that clean carpet with muddy boots, do you have to see the goal during the discipline? Yes. If there's a sibling rivalry among your children, should you see, even during their constant bickering, your will modification goal on the horizon? Yes.

"Cuthbertson, you've got to be kidding," you say. "You really expect me to be that objective during times of stress and tension?"

My response is a resounding yes.

If I'm having surgery, I want that doctor to be totally objective. I don't want his feelings to get in the way of what he learned in medical school. I want the mechanic to be objective when he is working on my automobile. I want the best of his knowledge, so that my car will run well. Likewise, our children deserve the best of our knowledge.

Tami was in some ways the hardest of our children to raise. Like me, she was more impulsive, more irritable. She became an excellent liar. She could look you in the eye and deny doing something even as the evidence was enclosed in her hand. Her expression would say, "How *dare* you suggest that I took the cookies!" God bless her, she probably had to write "I will not lie" about 10,000 times during her childhood.

Tami eventually went to Bible school and is now happily married, a mother, and a successful person. But I remember well when her will was modified. She was a sophmore in high school, and she had lied about something. I marched to school and pulled her out of class. We stood in the hall outside her room as she offered her defense. But then, for the first time in perhaps years, tears began to swell in her eyes. She broke down, sobbing, hugging me, and saying, "I'm sorry. Daddy, I am sorry."

At that point the bell rang, and kids came flying from the classroom.

There we were, father and daughter, hugging, and neither of us cared what anyone thought. That was a meaningful moment for us both.

I'm not going to imply that I had envisioned that moment back when she was refusing to eat her food at four years of age. But "discipline" without a goal does not lead to the kind of will modification Tami experienced that day.

Assertive Scriptural Parenting

Right attitudes plus right skills equal the right product. A breakdown of any of these can produce wrong results. Getting all three right might be called *Assertive Scriptural Parenting.*

Assertive speaks of purpose, decisiveness. If we understand the need for will modification and recognize the "bent" of each of our children, we have the confidence that leads to decisiveness. *Scriptural* reminds us that without apology we establish the Bible as our authoritative base. Inspired by God (2 Tim. 3:16), only the Bible has applicable principles (2 Peter 1:4) that can be *absolutely* trusted.

Let's follow the formula backward, starting with *right products.* All of us want to produce good "products" when it comes to parenting. But is success relative or absolute? One parent said, "I'm just thankful the kid didn't kill himself or end up in prison!" Certainly God's standard is above that.

Success is measured in one sense by *how our children view their training.* Your child is either saying, "I will not raise my children this way," or, "I hope I can do as well as my parents did." Proverbs 31:28: "Her children arise up, and call her blessed; her husband also, and he praiseth her." Can your children say that about you?

Success is also measured by *the degree of will modification.* Warnings on this subject are sprinkled throughout the Scriptures. Proverbs 17:2: "A wise servant shall have rule over a son that causeth shame." First Samuel 3:12-13: "In that day I will perform against Eli all things which I have spoken concerning his house; when I begin, I will also make an end. For I have told him that I will judge his house forever for the iniquity which he knoweth; because his sons made themselves vile, and he restrained them not." In 1 Timothy 3:12, presenting the qualifications for a deacon, Paul writes, "Let the deacons be the husbands of one wife, ruling their children and their own houses well." Ruling and restraining demand proper will modification.

In Proverbs 4:1-4, Solomon expresses appreciation for three aspects of a good upbringing: "Hear, ye children, the instruction of a father, and attend to know understanding. For I give you good doctrine, forsake ye not my law. For I was my father's son, tender and only beloved in the sight of my mother. He taught me also, and said unto me, 'Let thine heart retain my words: keep my commandments, and live.'"

Solomon is saying "Thank you" for good doctrine (v. 2), a wholesome relationship (v. 3), and proper instruction (v. 4). What doctrine are you sharing with your children? How are you sharing it? What is the relationship like between you and your children? Do you spend constructive time with them? Do they know they are important to you? What are you teaching them by word and example?

One way or another, child rearing has a product. My wife says, "You know, that boy of ours is just like you. You think alike, talk alike, even look alike." I think, *great.* We have spent hundreds of hours together, and I have shared with him my doctrine and teaching. I love spending time with him. With all due respect to my four girls, whom I love intensely, I have only one boy. Whom should he resemble, if not his father?

Right Goals
We are constantly teaching values, morals, and ethics to our children, whether we mean to or not. Every parent has a "philosophy of instruction."

My father said, "If you cheat a man out of a nickel, you cheat yourself." Now why did that stay in my mind all these years? Because it is a value he taught and lived. I have never cheated a man intentionally. Why? Because my father taught me.

My mother said to me when I was a young man, "Someday you will come across a fast woman. My counsel to you is to run away from her, not toward her." That thought was with me when I did run across a "fast woman." The value stuck. The result is that I have never had sexual contact with anyone but my wife.

Had my parents set no goals for my upbringing, it's doubtful that I would have taken these instructions so seriously. They would have been random proverbs. So even during the instruction stage, we parents need to keep asking ourselves, "What am I trying to produce?"

The Lord has goals for us during our times of correction. In Hebrews 12:5-15, words such as *chasten, correct,* and *scourge* are used ten times. The passage illuminates at least three goals God has in mind during these chastening times: (1) to help us give Him reverence (v. 9), (2) make us partakers of His holiness (v. 10), and (3) to cause our lives to manifest the "peaceable fruit of righteousness" (v. 11). Note that He is changing us for the better even as we're fighting the process. And, that's the way your children might feel toward you.

Proverbs 29:17: "Correct thy son, and he shall give thee rest; yea, he shall give delight unto thy soul." There are no greater gifts my children can give me than "rest" and "delight." After all, this raising of children is hard work, and I want to be able to rest someday! And what a delight it is to see that so many of those goals, I worked so hard to define were indeed reached. Why, I see them teaching the same values to *their* children! (Proverbs 17:6)

Right Skills

A former patient of mine had been punished when he was a child by being locked in his room for weeks. His parents would literally slide food under his door at "feeding time." Today he is a troubled adult. His poor behavior was stopped, but the method was wrong. His parents lacked the right skills.

Then there was the lady who, as a child, had been chained to the clothesline outdoors when she was disciplined. She would spend hours with a collar around her neck, running back and forth as the chain allowed. Her parents lacked the right disciplinary skills as well.

Both of these misdisciplined people were made to be strong-willed; both developed deep psychological problems. There is a fine line between modifying the will and making the child strong-willed, and the parents of these people crossed it. Here were wrong attitudes plus wrong skills plus wrong goals—and in both cases there were devastating products.

Dr. Bruce Narramore in his book, *Help, I'm a Parent*, distinguishes between punishment and discipline through this scenario:

Billy . . . had just pulled all the mixing bowls from the kitchen cupboard. Discovering the mess, Mrs. Martin said angrily, "How many times have I told you to stay out of there? You deserve a spanking!" With that she gave Billy a few good swats and sent him to his room. Head down and teary eyed, Billy headed for bed. Mrs. Martin was punishing Billy for his actions.

Contrast this with a similar scene at the Harris home. Little Raymond had just emptied the contents of mother's cupboard onto the floor. Arriving on the scene, Mrs. Harris said in a calm but firm voice, "Raymond, Mother has told you not to put the pans on the floor. Mother will have to spank you so you will remember not to do it again!" With that she gave Raymond a few good swats and said lovingly, "Now, let's help mother pick them up." Mrs. Harris was successfully disciplining her child.[3]

The difference may seem slight at first. But note how the attitude, skills, and goal all interweave. Sometimes it doesn't take much to "blow it."

Three Parenting Skills

It's easy to say that parents need the right skills. But exactly what kinds of skills do they need?

First, effective parents need the *skill of discernment*—the ability to tell what is going on beneath the surface of a confrontation. Undiscerning parents react only to the affront of being disobeyed. They think, *Who does this kid think he is? I am not going to have a child speak to me that way! I don't have to take that!*

I learned the hard way about emotional reactions when I was a student training in the adolescent ward of a state hospital. It was my first day there; I was going around in my little white aide's jacket, meeting people. I came upon a group of four boys playing pool and decided to attempt to "personalize" myself into their pool game. Suddenly one of the boys picked up a cue stick and whacked me across the back of the neck!

My first reaction was rage. I was tempted to break that stick over *his* head. But after I exited to an adjoining room and thought for a while, I decided I'd just learned a lesson. That boy was not only making it clear that this game was private; he was teaching me something about myself and my lack of skills. I had not discerned what was going on in that pool game.

Effective parents use the skill of discernment in at least three ways. They know the wisdom of these "pledges": (1) I do not want to react immediately to circumstances, I want to discern what is happening; (2) I must not get too personal with disciplinary words, because I do not want this situation to become a battle of wills; and (3) I must never use my child as a "whipping boy" for my own emotional needs. I will always be in control, especially during corporal punishment.

Second, effective parents have the *skill of communication*. We must remember that our words manifest what we are. We are modeling to our children a pattern of resolve, saying, "This is the way we deal with conflict in our home." Consequently, our words should be soft and quiet (Prov. 15:1; 1 Peter 3:4). Regardless of circumstances, the tone of voice is to be controlled.

This is hard, I know. In so many homes only extremes are manifested. Many of us grew up in homes where feelings were "acted out"; there was excessive yelling, anger, and rage. Others come from homes where feelings were kept inside; there was little communication. Breaking these patterns and substituting soft, controlled expression takes time and effort.

Furthermore, if we have something to say in disciplining our children, we should say it and be quiet (Matt. 5:37). Our tendency is to take every teaching circumstance as a chance to kick out our unresolved conflicts and pent-up hostilities. We go on and on with exaggerated tales of "When I was your age. . . ."

Finally, we should avoid using words that are destructive. Never use words like "hate" or "dumb." The words "shut up" should not be used. Our words should be edifying (Rom. 15:2; Eph. 4:29); they should build others up.

Alternative Discipline

Most of us tend to think of discipline as negative. But if discipline is defined as "the means by which a goal is reached," then the approach can be positive as well as negative. Rather than thinking only in terms of spanking, isolation, or denial of privileges, we can include two positive alternatives:

1. *Rewards.* If we punish bad behavior, we can reward good behavior. I worked hard for grades when my parents promised to give me $5 for an "A." I memorized Scriptures for pins and awards. You've probably had similar experiences.

In using rewards, we must be careful; not all children respond to them in the same way. But used properly, rewards can be incentives toward growth and development. Actions that are reinforced are more likely to be repeated in the future; behaviors that are not rewarded tend to weaken and disappear. This is a powerful weapon in the right hands.

2. *Explanation and praise.* All of us respond to warmth. It's easy for a father to forget that when he's busy and his son asks, "Dad, how

do you like my picture?" If the father takes time to comment favorably, he is reinforcing that child and disciplining him. As parents we need to be sensitive to such cues and to use them in training our children.

Some people find it hard to praise family members, even when the praise could improve a relationship. I have told couples in counseling, for example, that if they will give me ten minutes of their time daily, I can help change their marriages.

They stare in amazement. "You believe ten minutes will change our marriage?" they ask.

"Right. All I ask is that you get up ten minutes earlier, go down to the kitchen table, and sit there in your pajamas. Spend the first five minutes edifying one another; say nice things to each other. Then take the final five minutes to praise the Lord together. Tell God how much you love Him."

But some who have tried it have discovered that after the first couple of nice comments, they have nothing left to say. My response is to ask them, "Was that true in your last *argument*?"

Search for "points of praise" with your children. We all need "warm fuzzies." We all need to be "stroked."

3. *Varying activities.* Many studies show that children are strongly affected by television viewing. Many children's programs are quite violent; many espouse non-Christian values. The more we can establish that the center of the home is not in front of the "tube," the better off the whole family will be. Try to plan a wide variety of activities for your family, such as trips, reading, sports, board games, picnics, visiting museums—the list could go on. Keeping the kids active and interested will not only keep them out of trouble, it will enrich their growing minds and bodies.

Right Attitudes and Corporal Punishment
Skills and methods are useless without the correct attitudes. Ephesians 6:4: "Fathers, provoke not your children to wrath, but

bring them up in the nurture and admonition of the Lord."
Colossians 3:21: "Fathers, provoke not your children to anger, lest
they be discouraged." I shouldn't provoke; I should nurture. A nur-
turing attitude is especially essential when considering corporal
punishment.

Will spanking be part of your child's discipline or not? Parents
need to decide *before* misbehavior occurs how they will respond.
Scripture makes clear that a divided house will fall.

Because they deny the premise of the old nature, and because
they do not understand the biblical concept of will modification,
many popular doctors and psychologists condemn all physical punishment. Some call it "power assertiveness." Note this quote from
Child Psychology, a Developmental Perspective by William Meyer
and Jerome Dusek:

Power assertion refers to the use of physical punishment, the
deprivation of desired things or privileges, or the threat of these.
In using this form of punishment, the parent controls the child
through the child's weakness rather than through guilt arising
from the child's identification with the parent.[4]

From *Between Parent and Child* by Haim Ginott:

What is wrong with spanking is the lesson it demonstrates. It
teaches children undesirable methods of dealing with frustration.
It dramatically tells them: "When angry—hit." Instead of dis-
playing our ingenuity by finding civilized outlets for savage feelings, we give our child a taste of the jungle.[5]

In certain religious communities, meanwhile, spanking is not
only encouraged—it's overdone. There it is not a last resort, but the
first. In some cases the child is not spanked, but "whipped." I have to
admit that my blood chills when that term is used.

It is possible, however, to have a balanced view of corporal punishment. It is a means to be used properly in will modification. If a child does not need corporal punishment, don't use it. If it is needed, you as a parent must be in control of yourself when it is administered.

There are five places in the Book of Proverbs in which *rod* is mentioned in regard to discipline (Prov. 13:24; 22:15; 23:13-14; and 29:15). A rod was simply a stick cut from the stem or branch of a tree and used for various purposes, such as threshing (Isa. 28:27), as a staff of authority (Ps. 125:3), and to marshall and count sheep (Lev. 27:32, Micah 7:14). And, of course, it was an instrument of discipline.

Please note that it was *not* a belt. Under no circumstances should you hit your child with such an object. Nor was it the hand. You should not hit a child with your hand. I believe that a child will identify the punishment with the object; a parent's hand should have more positive associations. Perhaps a thin paddle might be the closest we can come to the biblical rod.

Corporal punishment should be used only when there is willful disobedience or malicious mischief. Be objective in your discipline, and be sure the child is aware of *why* he is being spanked. Discipline should be administered immediately after the offense; in fairness to Dad and to the child, Mom, don't say, "Wait until your father gets home!"

To summarize: Parents must establish a *philosophy* concerning corporal punishment. Passing feelings must not determine its use. Both parents need to agree on the purpose and method of discipline, and avoid fighting or bickering in the presence of the children. Parents should always be in control of themselves when disciplining their children—and should not make threats they have no intention of carrying out.

Basic to the Assertive Scriptural Parenting approach are parents with proper *attitudes* and *skills*. The goal is good *products*. Stop for a few moments and think. What are you doing right? What are you doing wrong? Are you keeping *goals* in mind as you discipline your children? Or are you recklessly administering punishments without thinking? Begin now to develop right attitudes and practice good skills, and you can begin to see good products.

5

Where There's a Will . . .

From where I sat in the living room, it was obvious that the boy was throwing things against the wall in his bedroom. The pastor had warned me about him. He was known to be incorrigible in church and school. The very mention of child rearing caused conflict between the parents. The pastor had asked me to call at the home.

Suddenly the boy realized that the door to his room was not locked. Out he rushed in all his glory, looking to be about seven going on eleven. He bolted by us in the kitchen, headed for the family room, and began to climb up a hutch. Glasses and china were crashing.

By the time the mother caught up with the boy, he had climbed up the hutch. She proceeded to "smack" him, and he went flying off the hutch into the wall. She grabbed him, placed him under her arm, and yelled at him without a pause as she literally threw him back into his room.

She then turned to me. "See?" she said. "I can't do a thing with this boy!"

That woman and her husband were not really raising their boy. *He* was raising *them*. All too many parents find themselves in this arrangement. In *Child Psychology, a Developmental Perspective*, William Meyer cites the following illustration:

Tommy begins to tease his baby sister; mother says, "Don't do that"; Tommy continues to tease; mother, somewhat louder, "Tommy, stop that"; Tommy continues to tease; baby sister starts to cry; mother yells loudly and slaps Tommy; Tommy stops teasing baby sister. These kinds of data almost force one to think interactively. Tommy is "teaching" his mother to escalate her response to yelling and slapping; the mother is providing a model of aggressive behavior and perhaps, somewhat paradoxically, providing reinforcement for his teasing by her dramatic display of attention.[6]

At least four types of parents are raised by their children:

- *The Helpless Parent.* "There is nothing I can do with that boy," says this type. Reaction to the child is characterized by helplessness and abdication of authority. "It's not my fault; I did the best I could."
- *The Competitive Parent.* "If I say it's black, he'll say it's white"; "I am not having a seven-year-old run my life." The parent regards the child's persistent defiance as a threat and moves into competition with the youngster, determined to show him who's boss.
- *The Inconsistent Parent.* "It seems these kids simply won't mind me." Because this parent has no philosophy of raising children, he is always experimenting with the youngster and finding much frustration. Because of these inconsistencies the child has difficulty knowing how to attain approval.

- *The Explosive Parent.* "This kid gets to me!" This parent is characterized by intense outbursts whenever he disapproves of the behavior of his youngster.

Turning the Tables

Parents do not *have* to be raised by their children, and they won't if they remember and follow these five guidelines for staying calm, compassionate, and in charge:

1. *Control yourself.* I do not agree with those who say our children should know that we are angry. But the children *should* realize *that they have done wrong.* True, they should be aware of our displeasure; but if ever there is a time when parents must be in control, it is during times of discipline.

One of the two Greek words for anger in the New Testament is the word *tumos.* This is a sudden, instant response; from it we get our word *tumult.* In Proverbs 16:32 we are challenged to rule our spirits rather than growing angry quickly. If we are going to be that rational about feeling anger, we can be rational about its expression as well.

This idea is reinforced by additional Scripture. Proverbs 15:1: "A soft answer turneth away wrath, but grievous words stir up anger." One result of responding softly in the midst of confrontation is that we gain a certain strength of objectivity. "Let every man be swift to hear, slow to speak, slow to wrath" (James 1:19). We get "confused" and turn those words around. Many of us are slow to hear, swift to speak, and swift to wrath. But it has been speculated that the reason God gave us two ears and one mouth is that He wanted us to listen twice as much as we talk.

Failure in this area is one reason for the battered-child syndrome that seems to be swelling in our society. In such cases children become scapegoats for unresolved problems in their parents. And as already noted, over-expression of emotions and too much discipline bring out the strong will in a child.

When a child does something wrong, you can be genuinely upset but absolutely in control of yourself and your actions. If you want to raise your voice, fine; raise it, but stay in control of your feelings.

2. *Use brief commands.* "Let your communication be yea, yea and nay, nay" (Matt. 5:37). When you have something to say, say it and be quiet.

"If I've told you once, I've told you a hundred times. . . ." Most children seem to have a little button behind the right ear that is turned off after the word "once." The in-charge parent does not get into the habit of haranguing or pleading through repetition.

3. *Develop in your child a "righteous fear."* Righteous fear is in between fear and respect. Your children must realize that when you say something, you mean it. When they are older and someone asks them what their parents were like in disciplining, they should be able to say, "When they said something, they meant it."

4. *As a couple, agree on the purposes and methods of discipline.* "Every kingdom divided against itself is brought to desolation; and every city and house divided against itself shall not stand" (Matt. 12:25). A child soon realizes how he can pit mother against father. If Mother says yes and Dad says no, and the child says, "Mom said yes," an argument between parents can ensue.

If my children ask me to let them go somewhere, my immediate response is, "Did you ask your mother?"

If they say yes, I ask, "And what did she say?"

"She said no," they say.

"Then why are you asking me?" I ask.

If their response is, "She said to ask you," then I understand that she wants me to make the decision. Otherwise, her decision stands.

5. *Develop a decisive method of discipline.* Anticipate your response *before* the action. As much as possible, envision your goal.

Two distraught parents approached me after a conference. "We can do nothing with this child," they said. "He does exactly the opposite of what we tell him." About this time, the seven-year-old son in question approached. He demanded their immediate attention. The parents, in turn, *pleaded* with the child for understanding.

"Can't you see, Johnny, we are talking with Dr. Cuthbertson?" they begged. "Please ... please ... please go and play ... *please.*" When the child finally left, I suggested that one doesn't *plead* with a seven-year-old; one exhorts, admonishes. There was little question about who was raising whom. Those parents needed to plan their responses and deliver them decisively.

Training Your Child

In our society many parents have more distinct conclusions about how to stop poodles from making puddles than they do about training their children. I suggest using the following four-step method of dealing with disobedience before your child reaches the teen years:

1. *Go over the problem with the child and review the consequences.* You need to know the consequences *before* the offense, so that you are not caught off guard. It would be good for all of us to look around our homes and ask ourselves, "What would I do if she broke the vase? What would be my response if he came through the back door with muddy shoes?" Every situation is a learning laboratory. Be thankful for the broken vase, thrilled at the muddy shoes. Here's a teaching opportunity!

"Surely you jest," you say. Not at all. The first step in dealing with disobedience is teaching. You are a teacher—that is part of having the proper attitude.

Let's take the proverbial cookie jar offense as an example. The child walks through the door and smells something delicious: chocolate chip cookies. Mom will not be home for a few minutes. The flesh says yes; the conscience says no. The flesh wins. The child walks over to the table, takes two or three cookies, and moves the rest around to make it appear as though nothing has been taken (that was *my* method, anyway).

Mom comes home and discovers what has occurred. She calls the child. Assuming that she wants this to be a teaching session, the dialogue might go something like this:

"Did you take the cookies?" she asks.

"Yes," replies the child.

"Honey, I don't want you to take the cookies because they are for supper. You will spoil your appetite." Note the instructional element. If the child has violated a biblical principle, the Bible should be opened and pertinent Scriptures shared with the child.

Mom continues, "Since I have made the cookies, you should ask me first. If you take the cookies again, you will be spanked." Note the consequences.

There are many alternatives for consequences, of course, including, "You will not go out" (denial of privileges); and "You will go to your room" (isolation). A parent should choose the consequences according to the seriousness of the offense and the psychological makeup of the child.

2. The second step could be called *feedback number one*. The child repeats to the parent what the latter has just said.

"Now, what did I just tell you?" says Mom.

"Don't get into the cookies," says the child."

"And what will happen if you do it again?"

"I will get spanked."

"Why shouldn't you get into the cookies?"

"Because they were made for supper and I will spoil my appetite."

Some children listen carefully and deliberately, but others have their minds somewhere else during the disciplinary process. A parent may have to repeat himself to a child two or three times to make sure the instructional phase is completed.

3. Now we move into the enforcement phase. *Follow through on the consequences.* If Mom has said, "If you do that again, you will be spanked," she will have to spank the child if he does it again. If she has said, "If you do that again, you'll have to go to your room for an hour," she will have to follow through. So when the child gets into the cookies again—and he probably will—she says something like this:

"What did Mother say would happen if you got into the cookies again?"

"I would get spanked."

The punishment ensues.

4. The fourth step includes *feedback number two* and *forgiveness.* After the child has been punished—perhaps after some cooling-off time has elapsed—Mom goes to the child and says, "Do you realize why you were spanked?"

"Yes," the child says.

"Why were you spanked?"

"I was spanked because I got into the cookies."

"Why shouldn't you get into the cookies?"

"Because they were made for supper and they will spoil my appetite."

Finally Mom looks at the child and says, "Do you have something to tell your mother?"

Without fail, my children always have said at this point, "I'm sorry. I was wrong."

The parent does not say, "Tell me you're sorry," or, "After all I've done for you ..." or, "If you really loved your mother...."

She says simply, "Do you have something to tell me?" Notice that by saying, "I'm sorry," the child is agreeing with the parent; values are being instilled.

After it is all over, Mom takes the child in her arms and says, "I love you, and I forgive you for what you have done."

To review: The parent (1) goes over the problem and explains the consequences; (2) has the child "feedback" this instruction; (3) enforces the consequences promised in step one; and (4) has the child "feedback" the reason for punishment and forgives the child. As this process of correction is followed, the child will learn discipline.

Guidelines for Pre-teens

To help your preteen child understand your expectations *before* an offense, try posting a set of guidelines on your refrigerator door. If possible, the entire family should be involved in establishing these guidelines.

The following is a suggested set of guidelines. Feel free to add, subtract, divide, or multiply according to your own situation. These are appropriate for most preteenagers; in the next chapter a similar approach for teenagers will be included.

GUIDELINES FOR DISCIPLINE
Preteenagers

1. *A chain of command will be respected.* This will start with Dad to Mom, and will go from the oldest to the youngest person. Rights and responsibilities will always be given to the oldest in charge. This must be followed by the younger children.
2. *The "Thumper principle" will be followed in communication.* That is, if you can't say something good, say nothing at all. The phrases "I hate you" and "shut up" will never be allowed. Swearing or "cussing" will not be allowed either.
3. *All problems will be resolved in the following way:*
   A. The parties involved will sit down and talk through their differences.
   B. If that is not successful, someone above them in the "chain of command" will help resolve this conflict. When this individual reaches a decision, the issue is settled.
4. *Teasing must be fun for all parties.* If it isn't, it must cease.
5. *In the discussion of issues, one person will talk at a time.* There will be no interrupting of one another.
6. *Hot and heated arguments will never be allowed.* Point three will be followed instead.
7. *At the discretion of Dad, majority rule can be followed.* This can be applied in such areas as watching TV, etc.
8. *When watching TV, if you leave your chair you may have it back on return—if you note that you are planning to return.*

9. *During the school year, bedtime for all children will be 10 P.M.*
10. *When discipline needs to be administered, it will be administered in this way:*
    A. Minor Offenses:
        (1) verbal reprimand
        (2) isolation in your room
    B. Major Offenses:
        (1) writing of sentences—in accord with severity and number of offenses
        (2) corporal punishment (spanking)—when there is willful disobedience or malicious mischief
11. *Dad will make all decisions unless power has been given to others in the chain of command.*
12. *Saturday morning will be cleanup time.* All jobs must be done by noon. If the job is not done, the person responsible will be subject to discipline.
    A. Fred—bathroom and kitchen floor
    B. Gina—living room
    C. Tricia—total cleaning of bedroom
    D. Michelle—toys and bedroom
    E. Gina/Michelle—lawn and snow

If your home is like mine, you may find these guidelines hanging on your refrigerator door forever—to be joined by the next chapter's guidelines when your children reach their teens.

6

Not Too Late for Teens

A lady said it well after a Family Life Conference. "You know, Dr. Cuthbertson," she said, "I am convinced that the only people really qualified to become parents are grandparents." She paused and I smiled. "If the Lord couldn't work that out," she continued, "at least we should have the option of throwing out the first two children." My smile turned to laughter. I knew exactly what she was saying.

She was saying this: Two people get married. They are young, inexperienced, getting to know one another, establishing jobs, striving to purchase a house, etc. Early in this process a child arrives—perhaps two.

Those parents think, *These children must understand that we are striving to survive.*

By the time the parents are ready to "surface," their infants have become teenagers. Now, as much more "serious" parents, they ask,

"Is it too late? We now have our homes; we are established in our roles and jobs. We are ready for parenting. Where are our kids?"

Remember Proverbs 22:6? "Train up a child the way he should go, and when he is old, he will not depart from it." In the Hebrew, the word for "old" refers to puberty. We are discussing the early teen years. By the time the child hits that age, the die is pretty well cast.

Thus the earlier you modify the will of your child, the easier it will be.

Are You Qualified?

Is it impossible to modify the will of a teenager? No; but it's harder. Before we examine methods for modifying the wills of teenagers, note these requirements for successful parents of teens:

First, *you must be willing to be "known."* Teenagers will demand a relationship of you. Your words must be backed by your actions, and those actions must be worth imitating. It has been said, tongue-in-cheek, that effective parenting of teenagers is 10 percent ability and 90 percent availability.

Are you capable of getting inside your teens' lives? Are you willing to do so? Many parents are incapable of doing that—and if the truth were known, they are not willing to pay the price to do so. Many of us are scared of "face-to-face" relationships; we are too insecure to really be known. Working with teenagers demands both.

Second, *you must be willing to express love and affection.* This is the number one psychological need for all of us. And 1 John 4:11-12 states, "Beloved, if God so loved us, we ought also to love one another. No man hath seen God at any time. If we love one another, God dwelleth in us, and His love is perfected in us."

If you are really trying to reach your teenagers, you have no choice but to love them. They will force you to do it. Oh, you might throw them out of the house; you might yell at them a lot; you might say how displeased you are with their present behavior. But if you really want to change them—if you really want to get a hearing—

the only alternative is to love them. If they sense your love and affection are sincere, they might even listen.

Learn to Negotiate

How can you modify the will of a teenager? By negotiating.

Let's say my son is enthralled by a television program, to the neglect of a chore. "David," I say, "you haven't fed the dog yet, and he is barking outside." The onus is put on David to respond.

He answer might be, "Dad, I will do it during the next commercial."

Aha, I think. *I've got him.* He has agreed that the feeding of the dog is his responsibility; he has agreed that he has not done it yet. And in the bigger picture, he is learning discipline. His will is being modified. I have just negotiated with him.

Proper negotiation demands the ability to give and take. It also demands mutual respect and the ability to communicate—which I define as the freedom to share questions, problems, and thoughts with someone else. The approach of the preteen years is no longer appropriate; the teenager must be viewed as a young adult.

In this negotiation process I am looking for any ground that may be given. Knowledge is power; I will be successful because I am aware of what's happening, and because I have developed skills accordingly.

Note that negotiation requires confrontation. Many parents are afraid of their teenagers. "I shouldn't confront them, I might lose them," these parents say. On the contrary; if you *don't* confront them, you will be *more likely* to lose them. The confrontation should be direct but tactful: "Would you give me some idea of why you came in late last night?"

The Pressure Principle

As you negotiate, learn to use what I call "the pressure principle." I didn't get this from a psychology book; I got it from the Bible.

As recorded John 8:1-11, Jesus was confronted with a woman who had been taken in the very act of adultery. In accord with their interpretation of the Law, her accusers were about to stone her. Jesus told them, "He that is without sin among you, let him first cast a stone at her" (John 8:7). Then silence ensued. Can you imagine standing in that crowd and having the Lord Jesus Christ simply looking at you? What would be the effect? "And they that heard it, being convicted by their own conscience, went out one by one, beginning at the eldest, even unto the last" (8:9). He had effectively dispersed the crowd.

This pressure principle, simply stated, means that whenever there is communication, the pressure of the words always falls on someone. To illustrate, let's return to the story of my son's promise to feed the dog. What if he didn't feed the dog during the next commercial? In that case I would move to confrontation and use the pressure principle. I would sit beside him, watching the TV also. My arm would be around his shoulder.

"Dave," I would say, "didn't you say you would feed the dog during the next commercial?" My next move depends on his next move. If he is apologetic and acts accordingly, the training is successful. If he decides to manifest a rebellious spirit, the negotiation moves to a different level—at which consequences are discussed.

Truth and Consequences: Three Levels

What happens when your teenager disobeys? There are three levels of alternatives depending on whether he or she is a "repeat offender":

1. *He decides; he chooses.* This is for the first offense. Your teenager has stayed out late or has not done a specific chore. You are aware of the need for will modification and are ready for confrontation. At this level you ask him, "What do you think would be fair punishment?" Remember, whatever he decides—within reason— you are buying. He wants to be treated as a young adult, and you are doing that. By letting him be involved in the decision-making

process, you are letting him aid the modification of his own will. But you always put this warning on the first step:

"Remember—the next time *I* will make the decision, if this happens again."

"But wait," you might say. "He'll catch on. He'll see that the first offense will always be easy to get out of." My experience has been the opposite. Young people like being treated as adults, and they know that if they aren't a little hard on themselves, you aren't going to buy the punishment.

2. *You decide; he chooses.* This is for the second offense. "Son, I told you that if you came in late again, I was going to make the decision," you say. "I want to be fair with you, so I will give you three options; You may choose one."

Ideally you have already made these choices since the first offense. You have chosen two alternatives that are harder and one that is easier. You are still treating him as an adult—and you are aware that he will choose the easiest of the three. You close this phase of will modification by saying, "Now, next time there will be only two options open to you. From these options, *I* will choose."

3. *You decide; you choose.* This is for the third offense.

As that teenager comes in late, he is aware of the consequences of his action. He knows that one of two hard options will be dictated to him. It's hoped that this not only serves as a deterrent to his actions, but that it also avoids intense confrontation. If you have made one of these options more difficult, you now have room for a bit of mercy if desired.

In all these cases, the "power" rests with the parents. They are striving to teach values, and are aware that the will modification of young adults is necessary to that teaching.

The Refrigerator Door
Just as the placing of guidelines for preteen discipline on the refrigerator door was recommended in the last chapter, so it is with teenagers.

Your young people are older now, of course, so the guidelines are different. But the purpose is the same. The following are only suggestions. The wisest course would be to establish your own, with input from both teens and parents.

TOP TEN TEEN GUIDELINES

1. *The "chain of command" will always be enforced.* This will be from God to Dad to Mom to the oldest child. When Mom and Dad are not around, the oldest child will be in charge and responsible.
2. *All differences must be quietly resolved.* The differing parties will discuss their differences until the problem is resolved. If mediation is necessary, Dad or Mom will be available.
3. *Others' clothes will not be worn without permission of the owners.*
4. *Disputes over watching TV will be decided by majority vote.* Dad will decide any ties. No questionable programs will be watched.
5. *There will be no dating of non-Christians.*
6. *No telephone calls are to exceed five minutes.* There must be a fifteen-minute waiting period between calls. Parents are exempt from having to follow this rule. Exceptions can be made from 10–11 in the evenings and at certain times on weekends.
7. *No negative or critical conversation is allowed.* The phrases "I hate you" and "shut up" are not to be used.
8. *Parents must know at all times where teens are.* There will be no curfew as such, but teens must get approval of all activities. When approval is given, the time for getting home will be jointly agreed on. Any change will require a phone call before the deadline.
9. *Discipline will be negotiated.* But continual violation of a rule will cause loss of this privilege.

10. *Ultimately God is changing us all.* He wants to move us toward righteousness and holiness (Heb. 12:10-11). May we all be continual students of our Father. To our teens: We ask for your prayers that we might have the wisdom necessary to raise you properly in the "fear" and admonition of the Lord" (Eph. 6:4). May God's love be shown and seen every day in our home.

7

When It Doesn't Work

She was belligerent when she came into my office. Her parents were making her seek counsel. She had been asked to leave two schools; the cut of her hair was "punk"; she was heavily into drugs, alcohol, and sex. Her two older sisters were both "super straight" and had attended Christian colleges. Her parents, who were fine, active Christians, were in a panic.

What happens when "it doesn't work," when will modification breaks down? In the case of this young lady, my role was relatively simple. I just had to establish a base of rapport, win her confidence, have the right attitude, and begin steps of instruction. Unlike her parents, I didn't have to be there when she first came in "stoned." I didn't have to chase all over the city looking for her when she decided to run away from home.

It is difficult to be objective when the rebellious child is our own. But we must try. The parent who responds incorrectly when things don't work will alienate the child, make the child stronger willed, frustrate himself, and possibly disqualify himself as part of the solution. If words lead to anger, and wrong actions lead to wrong attitudes, after a while a "divorce" occurs between parent and child. Pride makes it hard to be reconciled.

Make no mistake, however. When it comes to breakdowns between parent and child, God is consistent. Even though errors may have been made by the parents, God still upholds the child's responsibility to "honor your father and mother" (Eph. 6:2). The consequences of not doing so are devastating; the child "shall die" (Prov. 15:10); shall "be destroyed" (29:1); and is "the companion of the destroyer" (28:24). Under no circumstances does God excuse the actions of the child. The words of parents are still to be obeyed (Eph. 6:1).

Signs of Failure
The symptoms of failure are progressive; if the cause is not dealt with, the symptoms grow worse in six stages. The first symptom is (1) *nonverbal resistance* by the child—slamming doors, etc. Then comes (2) *verbal resistance*—talking back. This is followed by (3) *will resistance*, which means that the child wants his own way. Next is (4) *vengeance aggression*, when the child feels you deserve the pain. Then comes (5) *escape aggression*, in which patterns of avoiding reality are developed. Finally comes (6) *hostile aggression*, with the child striking the parents. Sometimes steps four and five are reversed or combined; in other cases step five is omitted.

On an attitude level, *rebellion* leads to *arrogance*, which leads to an *argumentative spirit*, which leads to *defiance*, which leads to *flight*, which leads to *hostility*.

Conflict is progressive. If you don't believe that, analyze your last "good" argument. It's amazing how, during domestic conflict, people can start with a relatively mundane disagreement—and before they are finished, they have "fried" the in-laws and are talking about divorce.

I observed a conflict recently at a local gas pump. A man's car had blocked a woman's from getting gas. The woman responded by calling the man a "moron."

He commented on her choice of words.

Her retort was that if he thought *that* choice of words was something, he should listen to *these*—and she swore a blue streak.

How should he have reacted to being called a moron? He could have said nothing; he could have apologized. But he *chose* to fight with her. She *chose* to fight with him, and the conflict escalated.

To see how this escalation works in the parent-child relationship, let's look in detail at those six downhill steps.

Stage One: Nonverbal Resistance
In this stage, the child resists discipline by slamming doors or communicating through such distinct body language as shrugging his shoulders. What does it all mean? Proverbs 15:10: "Correction is grievous [good for nothing] to him that forsaketh [turns from] the way: and he that hateth reproof shall die." The key is that the child is not responding to the discipline—the reproof—and is attempting to fight back. A reproof entereth more into a wise man than an hundred stripes into a fool. An evil man seeketh only rebellion" (Prov. 17:10-11). Note the correlation between reproof and rebellion.

I am assuming, of course, that the parents are not overly disciplining the child. I assume they are working hard at proper will modification.

Thus I am observing a child in rebellion, an obvious "flashing light" warning of trouble. Under no circumstances are the actions of this child "cute," or part of "growing pains," or "just a stage" he is going through. His will must be modified.

Note that the child is rebelling against reproof. His problem is universal. How do *you* respond when you are rebuked by your spouse or employer? Do you see tendencies toward a strong will in yourself? We live in a world of assertiveness, but as God has to modify our wills, we must do the same with our children.

The rebellious pattern must be corrected. If we accept biblical authority, we acknowledge that a child has an old nature that must be modified.

The tendency of "secular psychology" is to exaggerate the "goodness" of the child and to dismiss as environmentally caused those tendencies toward evil. But our society is plagued by social problems because of unresolved conflicts in *individuals*. Those conflicts can be traced largely to poor parental values established in children or to parents' failure to modify adequately the wills of their children—so that the children would be willing to accept their parents' values.

What can you do in this first stage? Always the first priority is to give love and affection and to try to understand what's going on in the child. "What can I do to help?" you might ask. "Can I hold you? Can we go somewhere?" Your attitude at this point is crucial. If you can appeal to conscience, do so: "This is hurting our relationship. I *need* you. I *need* to understand what is happening in your life."

Ideally, appeal and explanation will suffice. It must, however, be explained lovingly to the child that the disobedience must stop. If it does not, the child may slip to the second step.

Stage Two: Verbal Resistance

Now the child is talking back to his parents. Such behavior may seem funny on a TV situation comedy, but in real life it is not to be taken lightly.

I recall that just once as I was growing up I told my father to "shut up." I have never seen a man go into motion so quickly in my life! I had a hunch, as I was being lifted from my chair, that *perhaps* I had said something wrong. My father was not college-trained, but he understood will modification!

Arrogance and "talking back" to parents by children should never be allowed. "Whoso curseth his father or his mother, his lamp shall be put out in obscure darkness" (Prov. 20:20). The word *curseth* here means "being in contempt." The bitterness of rebellion has progressed to contempt.

The Bible makes clear the correlation of pride, arrogance, and words. "Talk no more so exceeding proudly; let not arrogancy come out of your mouth, for the Lord is a God of knowledge, and by Him actions are weighed" (1 Sam. 2:3). "Pride and arrogancy and the evil way, and the froward mouth, do I hate" (Prov. 8:13). "I will cause the arrogancy of the proud to cease, and will lay low the haughtiness of the terrible" (Isa. 13:11).

If a child is allowed independence prematurely, he can easily view himself—not parents, church, school, nor the Word of God—as the base of authority. It is easy for such a child to develop a strong will and to be demeaning toward others—including parents. Thus arrogance should not be allowed under any circumstances.

This is the crucial step as far as the "losing of the child" is concerned. If you use a quick, impulsive reprimand, you might drive the child away. But if you fear too much that your child doesn't like you and avoid doing anything, the child has found a means to control you. There must be a delicate balance here.

Giving love and affection and examining other concurrent factors in your child's life is important at this stage too. But the immediate goal is stopping arrogance. Use the methods mentioned in chapters 5 and 6—instruction for preteenagers, negotiation for teenagers.

If you have provided proper correction and affection, conflict should not have to escalate to the next stage. But if it does, professional help may be needed.

Stage Three: Will Resistance
Now begins a will-versus-will confrontation. Verbal resistance turns to arguing. Unfortunately, most of us have been there.

If a home is characterized by arguments and unresolved conflict, there should be no surprise when this is manifested in the children. In many homes Mom and Dad yell at one another; then, when the kids begin to yell, Mom and Dad yell at the kids. "We don't act that way around here!" the parents say.

The kids look at each other in amazement. Is it any wonder?

Proverbs 29:1: "He, that being often reproved hardeneth his neck, shall suddenly be destroyed, and that without remedy." Psychologically, the key to the passage is in the word *hardeneth*. The word means "to become tough, stiffen," or to become unmovable. The hardening individual is thinking, "I'm not going to take this; no one is going to push me around!"

If you observe that attitude in your child, you may be tempted to respond in like manner. If you do, the wills of both of you become more pronounced. "A brother offended is harder to be won than a strong city: and their contentions are like bars of a castle" (Prov. 18:19).

What is your success ratio for changing someone's mind in the heat of an argument? Not too impressive, I'd guess. Arguing is the *worst* way to change minds. If the person you're arguing with is telling you what a rotten no-good you are, are you saying "that's right! tell me more"?

No, you are probably waiting for a break in the words so that you can remind the other individual of his or her idiosyncrasies. By your example you are saying that arguing is acceptable. And you are forcing the other person to defend himself.

Verbal resistance can lead to will resistance, and arrogance can lead to an argumentative spirit. When this happens, parents and children can argue over anything—or nothing.

A lady asked me to counsel with her parents. "I am afraid for them" she said. "They have been married for thirty-seven years, and I am afraid they will kill one another. They argue all the time."

Sure enough, as those parents sat in the waiting room, they argued. During the counseling session I asked, "What do you argue about?"

"Anything," one of them said. "We go to bed arguing and we get up arguing. Many times we can continue in the morning where we were the previous evening."

What a way to exist!

If I develop an argumentative spirit, I will argue over almost any-thing. But that is not God's way. "The wrath of a king is as a messen-ger of death; but a wise man will pacify it" (Prov. 16:14). "The dis-cretion of a man deferreth his anger; and it is his glory to pass over a transgression" (Provr. 19:11).

What does it mean to "pacify" someone's wrath? What does it mean to "defer" anger? If I have a youngster who chooses to argue with me, I need to know.

The Hebrew word for "pacify" here means to tame or subdue. The word for "defer" means to put off till later. The implication is that with the right attitude and skills, I can "tame" the wills of my children; I don't have to respond angrily when I observe anger. I can defer it, thus having the ability to view the transgression differently.

With love and affection, then, I attempt at this stage to negotiate with my children. I will use corporal punishment here only if I be-lieve it will be productive. Hitting a child at this stage generally will not modify the will; it will make the child stronger-willed, which will be counterproductive. I want to tame the will. I will need to spend time with the child while maintaining a firm resolve to modify his will.

Stage Four: Vengeance Aggression

From this point the situation becomes increasingly severe and de-mands professional help. This stage is characterized by a pattern of *defiance*. At best the young person is saying, "You have it coming. Remember the time you hit me across the face? Well, now you're going to get yours!"

"Whoso robbeth his father and mother, and saith, it is no trans-gression, the same is the companion of the destroyer" (Prov. 28:24). At this point the young person's conscience has been weakened so drastically that he is saying things like, "Taking money from my par-ents is not wrong."

If you have ever harbored feelings of wanting to fight back, per-haps you understand. It's easy for certain people to internalize those feelings until those people become compulsive. It takes very little for the compulsion to lead to irrational behavior.

Once, while working as a chaplain in a juvenile home, I talked with a young man who had killed his mother.

"My old lady was on my back constantly," he declared. "I'd had a miserable day at school, and I thought to myself, *If she gets on my case when I come home, I am going to kill her.* Well, sure enough . . . from the time I came in the door I couldn't do anything right."

The young man had gone into the kitchen, picked out a butcher knife, and plunged the knife into his mother's back.

"Don't you understand?" he said to me. "I didn't have any other choice. If I had let her continue, I would have been destroyed."

Children at this stage are not necessarily homicidal, of course. But note the young man's mentality. His conscience was so weak that he could rationalize even the murder of his mother.

Defiance and vengeance must be dealt with professionally. This is not the time for yelling, screaming, or hitting. There might be room for negotiation; a trained counselor can help.

I hope that in your home the next two steps will not be reached. But if the will is not modified during infancy, childhood, or adolescence, only God can do it. There might come a time when you will have to let go and let God. You will have done all you can.

Stage Five: Escape Aggression

At this point the child, unable or unwilling to deal with reality, flees into fantasy. This is manifested through various self-destructive "flight patterns", including use of drugs and alcohol. This stage is very difficult for parents; professional help is needed—if the child will accept it.

In Luke 15 is recorded the Story of the Prodigal Son. It begins, "A certain man had two sons, and the younger of them said to his father, 'Father, give me the portion of goods that falleth to me.' And he divided unto them his living. And not many days after the younger son gathered all together, and took his journey into a far country, and there wasted his substance with riotous living" (vv. 11-13).

Note that the father gave money to *both* boys. Also note that he didn't yell at the younger son or even attempt to negotiate with him. He *let him go.* He was smart enough to *let him go.*

Parents, when it gets to this point, you cannot do what only God can do. If the child reaches this stage, you must be smart enough to let him or her go.

I believe it is more destructive to parents to try to keep such a child at home than it is to let him go. If you keep him, you have the possibility of continual confrontation and sleepless nights wondering where he is and what he is doing. Don't bring constant pain on yourself by refusing to let go.

After the prodigal son had fallen to his lowest point, he eventually "came to himself" (v. 17). That must be your prayer if your child reaches this stage. And just as the father was waiting with open arms when the repentant son returned, you need to be ready for reconciliation. It is one thing for that young person to make the decision to leave; it is something else for him to be "pitched out" permanently.

The prodigal son had a home to which he could return. So must your youngsters.

Stage Six: Hostile Aggression
At this final step, the child's open aggression can be seen. The young person is hitting his parents.

Proverbs 23:22: "Hearken unto thy father that begat thee, and despise not thy mother when she is old." The word for "despise" means to be disrespectful toward. Even in the worst home situations, most young people are still able to love their parents. Most end up saying, "My folks did the best they could." But some do not.

One young woman I counseled expressed adamantly and continually her hatred for her mother. Finally I stopped her and said, "I am going to accept for the moment that your mother is everything you are telling me. If she really is that bad, wouldn't it be better to be sympathetic toward her rather than hating her? She needs help. And if you carry this hatred, you are letting her problems become yours. She has been successful in bringing out the worst in you, and you have allowed it to happen."

It worked. But often when aggression turns to physical violence, professional help is declined. Sometimes there is no option but to call the police.

. One lady approached me after a conference. She was distraught; there were bruises on her arms.

"My problem is that there is no father in my home," she said. "My boy is heavily into alcohol and drugs, and when he comes home late at night, he will either put holes in the wall or hit me."

I volunteered to go to the home and attempt to reason with the boy. He came in fifteen minutes after we arrived. He was drunk, and proceeded to be very abusive to his mother and me.

When I tried to reason with him, he rushed at me, ready to fight. But his swinging first missed me because of his drunken condition. Then I rushed him and we both banged into the wall.

I was soon on top of him, holding down his arms. I looked into his eyes and said, "The next time you beat on your mother, I am going to suggest that she call the police."

Within a week, exactly that happened. As a result, the first serious counseling session with this young man was held in the county jail.

That woman's only recourse was to let her boy go, and to hope he would accept professional help. The latter would not happen until the physical abuse was stopped.

I trust your family will not have to suffer past the first two stages—nonverbal and verbal resistance. It is much easier to modify the will of a young child than to go through all this. How to modify that young child's will, keeping in mind the "bent" of that child, will be subject of the next few chapters.

8

As the Twig Is Bent . . .

A coach from our church was a model for me in high school. A former collegiate All-American, he had later played football with the Chicago Bears. On Saturday mornings some of us would gather at his school to be beaten by him in a sport of our choosing. I had deep respect for the man; he made a real imprint on my life. But neither of the coach's two boys was athletically inclined. The only time they got near the football field was when they played in the band.

I used to feel so sorry for that coach because he had those two sons. But I don't any more. Both boys developed into fine men.

God obviously meant for people to be different. Look at them on the street; there are tall ones, short ones, fat ones, skinny ones, intelligent ones, not-so-intelligent ones, ones with big feet, little feet, ridiculous feet. . . . There are athletic parents with nonathletic children, and vice versa.

Why? Is it "natural selection?" Or is God in it?

As we seek to raise our children, we may wish we'd been able to order brilliant, athletic, attractive, obedient offspring. But we have no control over what is sent to us. Who does?

One researcher has concluded that at birth there are some 4,500 predispositions in a child. Think of it! Besides physical differences, there are so many variations in personality and ability. Some children are docile, others aggressive; some learn readily, others do not; some are easily toilet trained, others are not.

Since J.B. Watson denied in the 1920s the role of heredity in determining behavior, the "nature-versus-nurture" (heredity-versus-environment) controversy has flourished. Is a child "born that way," or is he "raised that way"?

There is no need for an either-or choice here, however. Both heredity and environment interact with each other. In this chapter we will examine the inborn factors; later we'll look at environmental influences and how the two interact.

The Bent of a Child

We have already seen that Proverbs 22:6 may be paraphrased, "Modify the will of the child, the way he is bent, and when he gets to be a teenager, that pattern will stay with him."

Note that we must *modify the will according to the way the child is "bent."* Modifying the will of a compliant child will be much different from attempting the same with a defiant one. We need to understand the "bent"—the predisposition—of each of our children, as well as the source of that bent.

"Train up a child in the way he should go" (Prov. 22:6). That means in keeping with, in cooperation with, in accordance with the way he should go. The *New American Standard Bible* notes that the literal meaning is "according to his way." *His* refers to the child. The bent, or *way* of your child might be far different from your own. The *way* for the aforementioned football coach was sports. He had been genetically endowed with strength and athletic skills. His sons had not.

If you want to train your children with understanding and perception, observe each of them. Be sensitive and alert enough to discover each of their ways, and adapt your training accordingly.

That doesn't always come naturally. After a conference, a parent declared to me, "I have raised all my children the same."

My reply was, "I hope not. I hope you were sensitive to the bent of each of your children."

We can set similar standards and responsibilities for our children, but not identical aspirations and modes of training. A parent who lacks this sensitivity can have one child who turns out well, while another turns out badly.

Children and Arrows

The word for "way" in the Hebrew is *derek;* it means a "mode, manner, course of life." Psalm 11:2 uses this word to describe an archer bending his bow before he lets an arrow fly to the target. A form of the same word is translated "way" in Proverbs 22:6. The *Amplified Bible* translates this verse: "Train up a child in the way he should go [and in keeping with his individual gift or bent], and when he is old he will not depart from it."

Arrows are used to picture children in Psalm 127:3-5: "Lo, children are an heritage of the Lord: and the fruit of the womb is His reward. As arrows are in the hand of a mighty man; so are children of the youth. Happy is the man that hath his quiver full of them: they shall not be ashamed, but they shall speak with the enemies in the gate."

Why compare children to arrows? Well, what do you *do* with an arrow? You put it on the bowstring, grasp the bow, pull back the bowstring, and let the arrow fly. What a joy it is to see the arrow hit the target! What a beautiful analogy of "learning behavior" and the role of parents. You can work hard to get a good bowstring (all the knowledge you can attain). You can pull back that string as hard as you can (provide the right atmosphere, prayer, etc.). You can aim that arrow for the mark (have the right goals). And you can find great satisfaction when the mark is hit. What happiness there is for parents when their children rise up and call them blessed (Prov. 31:28). That is a result of Assertive Scriptural Parenting.

But arrows, like people, are not all the same. The parent must adapt to each child. My wife and I, for example, have five children with individual bents. As God has used knowledge of *our* bents to modify *our* wills, we as parents can use knowledge of our children's ways to modify theirs.

Accepting Our Children's Uniqueness

Once, while working with emotionally impaired children, I met Karen. She was a beautiful twelve-year-old, affectionate, dependent, and sensitive—but had limited intelligence. When she was frustrated she would "act out" her feelings in aggression and rage.

Her parents were both medical doctors. They were articulate, affluent, and strong-willed. They were determined that their kids would be intelligent and graduate from college.

They expected Karen to respond to these goals, but Karen could not perform to their expectations. They would not accept her obvious limitations. When she did not produce A's and B's on her report card, she was punished. On more than one occasion the parents took family vacations without Karen. She felt abandoned; crying for love, she became more and more enraged.

I believe that with different parents, Karen could have become a different child. Her mother and father would not accept her as she was—because they would not accept the fact that they had no control over the abilities of the child God had sent them.

God has established individual uniqueness. He meant for our children to be different from each other. We don't have to be guilty or bitter if one is handicapped or another is slow academically. I don't have to stay up nights wondering whether our children's differences are due to my wife's genes or whether I married the "wrong" person. God has given our children "designer genes."

God not only determines the inborn traits of individuals; He

For Thou hast possessed my reins: Thou has covered me in my mother's womb. I will praise Thee; for I am fearfully and wonderfully made: marvelous are Thy works; and that my soul knoweth right well. My substance was not hid from Thee, when I was made in secret, and curiously wrought in the lowest parts of the earth. Thine eyes did see my substance, yet being unperfect; and in Thy book all my members were written, which in continuance were fashioned, when as yet there was none of them.

Or, in the words of *The Living Bible:*

You made all the delicate, inner parts of my body, and knit them together in my mother's womb. Thank You for making me so wonderfully complex! It is amazing to think about. Your workmanship is marvelous—and how well I know it. You were there while I was being formed in utter seclusion! You saw me before I was born and scheduled each day of my life before I began to breathe. Every day was recorded in your Book!

Not only does God oversee the formation of each person; He also *purpose* in every birth. In 1 Corinthians 12:18, Paul speaks of relationship between the church—Christ's body— and our bod- "But now hath God set the members every one of them in the y, as it hath pleased Him." Verse 24 indicates that He "hath pered the body together." What does that say about *mistakes?* ere are none!

Environmental factors—such as use of drugs by the mother during pregnancy—can influence an unborn child. Even the effects of sins can be carried into future generations (Ex. 34:6-7). But the lt, the child, is God's creation. You may be brilliant but have gecally "slow" children. You may be an All-American football er but have a boy with two left feet. If you believe that God has a pose in all His creation, then you can believe He has a reason for gning your child differently from the way you might have.

views the entire concept of "good" and "bad" genes
skeptic who sees an "impaired" child says, "Why w
this to happen?"

God replies, in effect, "What *is* this? *I* have no
Hollywood prototype of success; *you* have. And i

When I was a teenager I visited a mental hospi
The ward for those with Down's syndrome made a
sion on me. Here were adults, forty and fifty years
liked me and asking me to hold their dolls. *What a*
doing with children's dolls? I thought. *What purpos*
all of this? I felt confused; I wanted to leave.

My panic illustrates how many of us are prone to I
azines, and television tell us who is beautiful, who
acceptable. But from God's perspective, there is
births of both "broken" and healthy people. As par
align ourselves with this principle.

The Sovereignty of God
God is totally aware of what is going on in the uni
surprised. Consider Psalm 139:1-2, 7-8:

> O Lord, Thou hast searched me, and known me
> my downsitting and mine uprising, Thou un
> thought afar off. . . . Whither shall I go from
> whither shall I flee from Thy presence? If I ascer
> en, Thou art there; if I make my bed in hell, be
> there.

God was there the day I fell out of a tree onto ce
over me as I was diagnosed as having a fractured skul
sion, and a possible blood clot on the brain. But Goc
had begun long before that. He had begun "weaving
ment of conception.

Consider Psalm 139:13-16:

Note in 1 Corinthians 12 God's attitude toward those in the church who seem less "presentable." As 1 Corinthians 12:23 indicates, "those members of the body, which we think to be less honorable, upon these we bestow more abundant honor." It would seem that God is not intimidated by the "Hollywood syndrome."

Your Child's Potential

As we understand that God has controlled the prenatal development of our children, and that He has established certain traits—a decisive bent—in each of them, we can see that He is aware of their individual potentials. This is true in terms of intelligence, emotional makeup, perception, and so forth.

But we parents can't just sit back and say, "Go to it, God!" He has entrusted our children to us so that we can train them. We are to be stewards, helping our children reach their psychological and spiritual potentials. We can do that by modifying their wills *according to their bents.*

In the final analysis, God is even more concerned about each of our children than we are. After all, He *did* make them. He has given them not only the potential to grow, but to teach us as they do.

Evangelist John Haggai, with tears streaming from his cheeks, publicly thanked the Lord one day for his retarded child. "The Lord has used this," Haggai said, "to give me sensitivity that I would not have had otherwise."

Remember, God is changing *our* wills too.

9

One of a Kind—but What Kind?

God has placed a "bent" within each child, as seen in the previous chapter. The challenge for parents is to modify the will in keeping with the bent. For example, harsh discipline for one child might be effective—but for another, devastating. One child might be very responsive to love and affection and another unresponsive.

From this we can surmise why two children raised in the same environment might be so different. They respond in different ways to discipline because God has placed different bents in them.

Let's review the basics of Assertive Scriptural Parenting. The will must be modified because each child has an old nature. This old nature puts the child in a state of rebellion, bends him away from God, and causes him to miss the mark of God's righteousness. We have listed some methods for modifying the will, based on the premise that the right attitude plus the right skills lead to the right product.

We have also established that the will is to be modified in accord with the unique bent placed in each child by God. To do that, we must define as clearly as possible the kinds of bents children have. This chapter will do precisely that.

The Bent: An Example

It didn't really hit me until I was sitting in the car in front of our house one Sunday morning, honking my horn. That's when I saw how my wife and I have different bents. She is a *sensitive* person—and slow and methodical. I am an *irritable* person, quick and somewhat impulsive. Preparing for church on Sunday morning was as good a battlefield as any on which our bents could clash. I wanted to hurry, to get to church on time. My poor wife, on the other hand, wanted to be sure our children looked proper and that no detail had been overlooked.

Why couldn't she have started sooner? I thought. *Why isn't she like me?* It just didn't enter my mind that I could have stayed in the house and helped with the children. It was so much easier to sit in the car and lean on the horn.

I have since concluded that the biggest obstacle to oneness in marriage is this difference in temperaments, or bents. If I came rushing home from work, for instance, and suggested that we immediately leave for a canoe trip down the Colorado River, I would be met with resistance. I would put up the same resistance if she suggested that the two of us run a day care center.

God has given us different bents. She is sensitive; I am irritable. But God wants me to change through interacting with my wife, and He wants my wife to change through the same process. Similarly, it is no mistake that God gave us the children we have. He wants us to learn from them. So I must not try to fight those differences in temperament; I am to learn from them.

The Nature of Temperament

Temperament may best be viewed as the *how* of behavior. Two children may be able to throw a ball with accuracy and have the same motives in doing so. Yet they may differ with respect to the intensity with which they act, the rate at which they move, the moods they express, and the readiness with which they shift to a new activity. They may also differ in the ease with which they approach a new toy, a new situation, or a new playmate.

Temperament is the behavioral style of a child—the *how* rather than the *what* or *why*. Technically, it can be defined "the characteristic tempo, rhythmicity, adaptability, energy expenditure, mood, and focus of attention of a child, independently of the content of any specific behavior."[7]

Temperament is not unchangeable. Like any other characteristic of an organism, its features can develop and be significantly affected by environmental circumstances. Few adults are aware of how this nature-nurture interplay has affected them; they don't stop to think, *Was I a defiant youngster? Is there a correlation between that and my aggressiveness now in business? Was I a sensitive child, and is that why I still have such a difficult time meeting people?*

Doctors Alexander Thomas, Stella Chess, and Herbert Birch once studied the temperaments of 141 children from thirty-five families over a period of ten years. They summarized their conclusions in their excellent book, *Temperament and Behavior Disorders in Children* (New York University Press).

They recognized that "temperament cannot be the heart and body of general theory," but felt that "we must give as much attention to temperament as environment."[8]

Chess, Birch, and Thomas concluded that a child has genetic predispositions in nine areas, descriptions of which follow. Try to analyze how some or all of these factors are manifested differently in each of your children. Then try to identify your own traits in these areas. Differences between you and your children may explain in part why confrontations have occurred.

1. *Activity.* This describes the level, tempo, and frequency of the child's movement. Does your child move around a great

deal? Did she crawl all over the house? Or was your child inactive? Are you as an adult an active person? Are you impulsive? Do you react slowly or quickly to stimuli?

2. *Rhythmicity.* This refers to the degree of regularity of repetitive biological functions, including rest and activity, sleeping and walking, eating and appetite, bowel and bladder function. Does your child demand a regular nap each day? Does he want to be fed at the same time each day? Were you systematic as a child? Are you now?

3. *Approach or withdrawal.* This describes the child's reaction to any new stimulus—food, people, places, toys, or procedures. When you took the child to the doctor for the first time, did he cry? Does he warm up to people easily? Did he like new toys? Do you warm up to new people easily? Do you withdraw from new situations and people?

4. *Adaptability.* The emphasis here is on the ease or difficulty with which the child's responses can be altered. Did the child show low flexibility by holding himself stiff for a long period when he took a bath? Is there some food you didn't like as a child and still don't?

5. *Intensity of reaction.* In this category, interest is directed to the energy content of the response, regardless of direction. A negative response may be as intense or mild as a positive one. Did your child scream a lot? Did he laugh loudly? Were you a demanding child in this way?

6. *Threshold of responsiveness.* This refers to the level of stimulation necessary to evoke a response. Was your child easily startled? Would she wear dirty diapers for long periods with little response? What is your threshold now as an adult? Does it take a lot to get you upset?

7. *Quality of mood.* This describes the amount of pleasant, joyful, friendly behavior as contrasted with unpleasant, unfriendly behavior, as well as crying. Did your infant cry for ten minutes before he would go to sleep? Did he always

smile at strangers? Were you a friendly child? Were you always picking fights as a kid?

8. *Distractibility.* This refers to the ease with which the child's ongoing behavior may be interfered with or changed. Did your child stop crying when you picked her up? If he was crawling toward danger, would the shaking of a rattle divert his direction? Are you easily distracted today? When you set your mind to accomplish something, do you stay with it?

9. *Attention span and persistence.* This includes the length of time a particular activity is pursued. Did your child play with a toy for long periods? Could you leave him by himself, knowing he would amuse himself? If you are hearing a sermon, is it easy for the pastor to get and hold your attention?

We can take all or any of these categories and note the differences among our children. As already mentioned, one researcher suggested from his studies that there could be 4,500 variable, prenatally set traits. I contend that from God's perspective, this is only scratching the surface. Perhaps there can be 4,500 differences in mood, 4,500 differences in adaptability, or 4,500 differences in rhythmicity, and so on! After all, science has only discovered a fraction of what God has created. But the more we know about our children's "bents," the better we will be as parents.

Chess, Birch, and Thomas identified three different temperaments—the easy child, the slow-to-warm-up child, and the difficult child. I would like to propose four categories: (1) the *defiant* child, (2) the *irritable* child, (3) the *sensitive* child, and (4) the *compliant* child. Here is a scenario of the "bents" and an inventory to help you determine which applies to each of your children.

The Defiant Child
The defiant child is a challenge on any day. He is a difficult child to raise. Here are some of his characteristics.

- He acts out his feelings. Many times he laughs or cries loudly.
- He usually responds negatively to new stimuli. It seems you can never please him.
- He is constantly striking out at others.
- He is slow to adapt to changes in the environment.
- His mood is often negative and his reactions intense.
- His biological functions are irregular. He may awaken at unpredictable intervals; his hunger may be irregular.
- He spits out his food.
- He cries more than he laughs. He shrieks more than he whines.
- He has a pattern of slow adaptability.

In studies done by Chess, Birch, and Thomas about 4 percent of the children fell into the similar "difficult" category. Some who later emerged with leadership qualities were in this group; but, about 23 percent of the behavior problems in the study were also here. Defiant children have the potential of being "real good" or "real bad." Parents with defiant children need to provide the proper environment to foster the "good" in the child.

Parents with defiant children often feel very guilty. They may have to fight feelings of wanting to reject the child or the feeling that God is punishing them through the child. But loving, compliant parents don't always have contented children.

If your child is defiant, be careful about responding impulsively to him. Wrong responses could be devastating. Force against force with a defiant child can produce a very strong-willed youngster. Further guidelines on dealing with this type of child will be presented later.

The Irritable Child

The irritable child can be awfully hard to please. If you sit him one way in the crib, he wants to be sat some other way. If you feed him one thing, he wants to be fed another. Here are some of the irritable child's characteristics.

- He is very determined to get his own way.
- He has a strong desire to get what he wants. This might be expressed as determination on the positive side and stubbornness on the negative side.
- He is generally not overly responsive to affection.
- He is generally a very active child. He wants to explore; he is a crawler.
- His sleeping and eating patterns are not regular.
- This child is easily distractible.
- He is generally persistent in things that are important to him.
- He is often harder to lead than other youngsters, and he is more cautious about who he follows.

The irritable child seems to be more set than the defiant child. Whereas the defiant child might act out his feelings, the irritable child can put his will against yours without even flinching. The will of the irritable child is best met with love. The defiant child might meet your attempts of affection with hostility, but the irritable child has more difficulty hurting someone who really seems to care. If you try to break his will with force, he might fight you.

I recall a woman coming to me for counsel and stating, "My problem is my son. He beats me up."

"Beats you up?" I said. "How old is this boy?"

"Eight," she replied, "He kicks me and beats on me when I lie down. What am I to do?"

I learned that the boy's father had left the family about a year before, and there had been a difficult divorce. I went to meet the boy, and I will never forget his greeting at the door. Before I had said a word, he demanded, "Who are you? What are you doing here? I don't like you."

I picked him up and sat him on a chair. "You don't talk to me that way. I understand you have been beating on your mother. It has got to stop—do you understand? Now tell your mother that you are sorry." He squirmed, moved toward his mother, and apologized.

When he returned, I continued, "I love you—do you know that?"

The story has a happy ending. Even though he was attempting to punish his mother for letting his father go, in my judgment, he was not a defiant child. A surrogate father was found who befriended the child, took an interest in him, and loved him, and the boy is responding well.

The Sensitive Child

The sensitive child can be the most dependent of the four, which can be good or bad depending on how the parents respond. Here are some of the sensitive child's characteristics.

- He demands much attention and affection.
- The first contact with strangers usually causes him to turn away or cling to the mother.
- He generally has negative responses to new situations.
- In new situations, he withdraws at first and adapts very slowly.
- His activity level is usually low or moderate.
- His moods are characteristically mild, so that his initial negative reaction is quiet.
- He is slow to accept new people.
- He can easily develop feelings of depression and loneliness.

The wise parent with a sensitive child combines patience with a willingness to wait. Because of his high dependency level the sensitive child will desire a close relationship with a parent who moves cautiously. If the child is pushed too far too fast, a battle can ensue.

Some parents become impatient with a youngster who avoids new experiences. There are two dangers for these parents. They may put too much pressure on the child with repeated insistence on participation, or they may not provide the youngster with the repeated exposures to new experiences that will allow the child to adapt and become comfortable.

I remember a little girl I first met at a church camp many years ago. At every meeting when I spoke, she seemed to stay on the edge of the group by herself. It was obvious that she had few friends. Not thinking in terms of temperament, I determined that I was going to "break down" this young lady. I was sure that she was lonely, so I was determined to get into her world. When I finally cornered her, I did all the talking. She was hesitant to answer my questions. Finally, a breakthrough took place. This little girl is now a young woman with whom I still correspond, and she still shares with me. She has given to me the privilege of knowing her world. My attitude toward her has shifted, however. I have grown to realize that she will never be loud or the life of the party; she doesn't have to be and doesn't want to be. Her temperament is not that way.

The Compliant Child
This child is every parent's dream. He is a good baby and with the right environment an easy child to raise. These are some of the compliant child's characteristics.

- He is generally positive in mood.
- He is highly regular in his eating, sleeping, and bowel patterns.
- The intensity of his reactions is low or mild.
- He is rapidly adaptable and unusually positive in his approaches to new situations.
- He smiles and laughs more than he cries.
- He generally evokes pleasant responses in other people.
- As he grows older, he will have the tendency to be positive and find good in life and things.
- He is a comfort to other people.

One might think that compliant children would never have any problems. Chess, Birch, and Thomas develop two possible negative behavior trends. The first is that they could be highly susceptible to trauma. Because of their compliancy, they can easily develop lower defenses than other children. When crisis, responsibility, or stress occur, they may have extra difficulty with it.

The second trend is that their virtues can turn to vices. These children easily copy the rules, regulations, mores, and manners of their parents, sometimes exaggerated to the point of caricature. But they also need acceptance from their peers. The mores of the peer group might differ from those of the parents. Usually, the child can adapt to both, but if the patterns of the parents are inconsistent or the parents tend to dominate the child, he might feel a stronger attachment toward his friends. He too has a sin nature.

Here are a few questions to think about in closing:

- Do you respond differently to each of your children?
- Have you attempted to define why each of your children are different?
- Are you able to acknowledge that God has given a different "bent" to each of your children?
- Are your children's traits different in the nine areas mentioned in this chapter?
- Which of the four temperament patterns defined in this chapter seems to fit each of your children?

The following inventory was established to aid you in determining the bent of each of your children. I would encourage you to take it individually for each of them.

CUTHBERTSON CHILD TEMPERAMENT ANALYSIS INVENTORY

This inventory is designed to aid you in further understanding your child. It will help you measure six traits and four temperament patterns for your child. If you have more than one child, complete the inventory separately for each one.

You will have thirty observations to respond to about your child. These are generally measured in terms of intensity, so special care should be taken to be as objective and precise as possible. In each item, rank the lettered responses from 1–4, with 4 corresponding to what would be the most typical behavioral pattern for your child, and 1 corresponding to what would be the least typical behavioral response for your child.

1. During the pregnancy, the child was:
   _____ A. extremely active.
   _____ B. active.
   _____ C. occasionally active.
   _____ D. relatively inactive.

2. Which of the following corresponds most closely to the child's napping habits?
   _____ A. He was very restless; he would often awaken and have trouble getting back to sleep.
   _____ B. His naps were irregular.
   _____ C. He would want to be held or know that someone was close during nap time.
   _____ D. His nap patterns were regular; at the same time each day he would be sleepy and would generally fall asleep no matter where he was.

3. When meeting new people, his reaction was:
   _____ A. negative.
   _____ B. irritable.
   _____ C. to warm up very slowly.
   _____ D. to warm up fairly quickly.

4. When the child was hungry, he tended to:
   _____ A. cry continuously.
   _____ B. cry off and on loudly.

_____ C. cry softly.
_____ D. show a minimal amount of displeasure.

5. In general, the child was:
_____ A. very discontented.
_____ B. fairly discontented.
_____ C. fairly contented.
_____ D. very contented.

6. Which of the following best describes the child's patterns of accepting physical affection?
_____ A. generally resisted being held for long periods of time
_____ B. sometimes resisted being held, sometimes co-operated
_____ C. demanded to be held for long periods of time
_____ D. seemed to be fairly content whether he was held or not

7. During the night the child usually:
_____ A. was extremely restless.
_____ B. was restless.
_____ C. had restless periods, but normally moved around very little.
_____ D. moved around little.

8. By age one, how had the child adjusted to an eating and sleeping schedule?
_____ A. He resisted attempts to get him on a regular schedule.
_____ B. He would follow the schedule but was fussy and would fight it on occasion.
_____ C. He would generally follow a regular schedule.
_____ D. He would consistently follow a deliberate schedule.

9. When faced with new foods, the child:
_____ A. would be defiant, often crying or throwing food.
_____ B. either liked new foods readily or not at all.
_____ C. responded fairly favorably, although he did seem to want his special plate or spoon.
_____ D. responded generally very well.

10. How sensitive to noise was the child?
_____ A. very sensitive
_____ B. fairly sensitive
_____ C. fairly insensitive
_____ D. very insensitive

11. When your child disliked something, to what extent did he let you know?
_____ A. He was very demonstrative.
_____ B. He was fairly demonstrative.
_____ C. He was fairly nondemonstrative.
_____ D. He was nondemonstrative.

12. How easily was your child distracted from crying?
_____ A. He resisted toys or activities and continued to cry.
_____ B. He was easily distracted.
_____ C. He responded to certain toys but resisted others.
_____ D. He was generally responsive to any toys given to him.

13. How did the child respond to taking naps?
_____ A. I had an extremely difficult time getting the child to take naps.
_____ B. The child was normally willing to take naps but sometimes had difficulty getting to sleep.
_____ C. The child took naps but many times demanded that he be rocked or held.
_____ D. The child readily took his nap.

14. To what extent does each of the following correspond to the child's bowel and diaper patterns?
_____ A. His bowel movements were irregular.
_____ B. He did not like wearing dirty diapers.
_____ C. The child's bowel movements were fairly regular, and he was fairly good about wearing soiled diapers.
_____ D. His bowel movements were regular, and he did not seem to mind wearing soiled diapers.

15. When given his first bath, he:
_____ A. responded violently.
_____ B. responded cautiously.
_____ C. reached out for support.
_____ D. responded well.

16. How did the child react to different clothing fabrics?
_____ A. The child reacted violently to certain fabrics.
_____ B. The child would fuss and be irritable if fabrics bothered him.
_____ C. The child would accept a fabric that might be irritable with a minimum of visible discomfort.
_____ D. I can't recall the child acknowledging that a certain fabric was uncomfortable.

17. How responsive was the child to affection?
_____ A. unresponsive
_____ B. unresponsive on occasion
_____ C. consistently responsive
_____ D. responsive on occasion

18. How long would the child generally play with a toy?
_____ A. for a very short period of time
_____ B. for fairly short periods of time
_____ C. for fairly long periods of time
_____ D. for very long periods of time

19. How active was the child during the first five years?
_____ A. The child was extremely active during the first five years.
_____ B. The child was an active child and occasionally resisted settling down.
_____ C. The child wanted to stay close to his mom.
_____ D. The child was not overly active during the first five years.

20. To what degree does each of the following describe the child's playtimes?
_____ A. His playtimes were selfish; he played with what he wanted, when he wanted it.
_____ B. His playtimes were erratic; certain toys just would not be acceptable to him.
_____ C. He always had a favorite toy and would play with it consistently.
_____ D. He was fairly consistent in playing by himself and with a variety of different toys.

21. When left with a baby-sitter, the child
_____ A. was defiant and uncooperative.
_____ B. was fussy but cooperative.
_____ C. might cry when left but was generally cooperative after that.
_____ D. was cooperative.

22. When my child was upset, his most typical reaction was:
_____ A. loud crying much of the time.
_____ B. loud crying sometimes.
_____ C. squeaking and fussing.
_____ D. whimpering and fussing.

23. In general, how would you describe the child's mood?
_____ A. very uncooperative
_____ B. fairly uncooperative
_____ C. fairly cooperative
_____ D. very cooperative

24. If a toy were out of reach and he wanted it badly, the child would:
_____ A. cry and be demonstrative until he finally got it.
_____ B. make every effort to get the item on his own.
_____ C. fuss momentarily and be reconciled to the fact that he was not going to get the toy.
_____ D. realize that he couldn't get it and move on to something else.

25. How did your child respond to diaper changing?
_____ A. He moved around so much that it was hard to change his diaper.
_____ B. He did not like dirty diapers and was vocal about it.
_____ C. He could tell when there was a new type of diaper or new powder and did not take well to these changes.
_____ D. The child was always cooperative at changing time.

26. As to his daily habits (eating, sleeping, bowel movements), how would you describe the child?
_____ A. very unpredictable
_____ B. fairly unpredictable
_____ C. fairly predictable
_____ D. very predictable

27. When visiting friends or relatives, the child often:

    ———— A. broke something, cried loudly, or had some other problem before going home.

    ———— B. was fussy and irritable at some point.

    ———— C. got along with everyone and did not create any problems.

    ———— D. wanted to stay close to his mother and did not take to new people readily.

28. If the child was playing and heard a loud noise, he would be most apt to:

    ———— A. be startled; his behavior would change almost immediately.

    ———— B. want to investigate the source and respond to it.

    ———— C. be scared and look to a parent for support.

    ———— D. look up but soon resume playing.

29. How easy was it to tell if the child did not like something?

    ———— A. very easy

    ———— B. fairly easy

    ———— C. fairly difficult

    ———— D. very difficult

30. If someone chose to direct the child's attention to something else, he would:

    ———— A. resist this and keep on doing the same activity more deliberately.

    ———— B. resist this and be annoyed at the interruption.

    ———— C. stop his activity and move slowly toward the new one.

    ———— D. stop his activity and be fairly delighted at the new one.

Scoring

Each item on the inventory concerns one of the six traits, as shown below.

(1) Activity level—items 1, 7, 13, 19, 25

(2) Rhythmicity level—items 2, 8, 14, 20, 26

(3) Adaptability level—items 3, 9, 15, 21, 27

(4) Threshold level—items 4, 10, 16, 22, 28

(5) Mood level—items 5, 11, 17, 23, 29

(6) Distractibility level—items 6, 12, 18, 24, 30

Each response (A, B, C, and D) is correlated with one of the four temperament patterns.

A—Defiant

B—Irritable

C—Sensitive

D—Compliant

Step 1
For each trait, add up your numbered responses (1–4) for each temperament (A, B, C, and D). Note this example.

ACTIVITY LEVEL

Item #	A	B	C	D
1	4	3	2	1
7	3	1	4	2
13	4	3	2	1
19	2	3	4	1
25	4	2	3	1
TOTAL	17	12	15	6

After you have done this for each of the six traits, you will know the child's dominant temperament pattern for each trait. In the example given, the child's dominant temperament pattern for activity level is *defiant*, since A had the highest score.

Step 2

To determine the dominant temperament pattern overall, add together all the A responses for all the traits, then all the B's, C's, and D's, as shown in the example.

TEMPERAMENT DETERMINATION

Trait	A	B	C	D
Activity	17	12	15	6
Rhythmicity	18	13	10	9
Adaptability	20	12	13	5
Threshold	22	12	12	4
Mood	21	9	15	5
Distractibility	23	10	15	2
TOTAL	121	68	80	31

The child represented by the example falls into the *defiant* category, since column A has the highest score.

10

The Parent-Child Match

If the goal is to modify the child's will in accord with his bent, then at least one other variable needs to be measured, namely, the parents' temperaments and the home environment they create. Two strong-willed parents will raise a defiant child much differently than would two weak-willed parents. As we have discussed the modification of the will and individual temperaments, we have seen that each specific of each child is important. We must give attention to what we are rewarding and punishing, the timing of punishment in relation to what the child does, the degree of frustration involved, the clarity with which expectations are communicated to the child, the consistency of discipline and reinforcement, and so on. But it also makes a difference who we as parents are.

A woman I'll call Mary came to me for counseling. She had been raped by her father at the age of twelve; she became pregnant (by another man) and had an abortion at seventeen. Mary was married to the father of the aborted child for about two months before they split. Her own father had convinced her that she was the reason that he and her mother had broken up. From the ages of eighteen to twenty-four she lived with another man, and that relationship eventually died. At twenty-four she became pregnant by yet another man. After having the child, she was rejected by that man. At this point, she gave up. I believe that subconsciously, she decided to die. Since she didn't have the nerve to put a bullet in her head, she decided to starve herself to death. When I first met her as a patient, she was 5'9" and weighed only about eighty pounds. I was impressed by her from the beginning—here was a beautiful, sensitive girl who never had a chance. What a joy to see her life completely turn around! As a matter of fact, the Lord not only turned her life around, He "flipped it over." But first she had to overcome some bad parental training.

To understand why some kids "go bad" and become throwaways in our society, let's look at how the environment we parents create interacts with the child's temperament.

Environment Interacts with Temperament

As Chess, Birch, and Thomas state, "Environment and temperament are not completely independent entities. Environment and temperament not only interact, but they also *modify each other*. A parent's attitudes toward and practices with a specific child may reflect preexisting, long-standing aspects of the parent's personality structure. But, these attitudes and practices may also be reactive and reflect a response to the temperamental characteristics of the given child"[emphasis mine].[9] What's being said is this: how I react to my child is due partly to my own temperament and partly to the way my child's temperament and mine interact. Most of this is subconscious. Most of us don't realize temperament differences between us and our spouses. Most of us until now have not analyzed our children's temperaments. Most of us don't realize that different environments and different parenting philosophies do react differently to the different temperaments of our children. But there are many ways environment can modify temperament.

A naturally negative child may become more positive if the environment is gentle and favorable. If our children are defiant or irritable, wouldn't it be better to give love rather than meeting force with force? I think the human tendency is to think, *I'll show them. I'm not going to be pushed around.* Then things get worse, and we often become negative and embittered ourselves. Calculate your strategy and modify that behavior through love.

A very adaptable child may become hardened in a hostile home. If two strong-willed parents have a very sensitive child, they must be careful not to "break the spirit with the will." If your children feel you are being unreasonable, they will subconsciously look for ways to fight back. If you are strong-willed and religious, for instance, your children know that they can destroy you with the simple words, "I *don't want* to go to church." They couldn't hurt you more with a two-by-four.

A defiant child can become intolerable with excessive discipline. If I meet force with force, I may make the child uncontrollably strong-willed, rather than modifying the will of that child. *Excessive* discipline can bring out the worst of the bent.

Not only can the environment affect the temperament, but the temperament can also affect the environment. For example, a child who is difficult to care for can affect how a parent responds. Few things can challenge a sensitive mother more than having a defiant son. She wonders constantly, *why?* She recognizes her position and feels defeated and locked in. She may as a result approach child rearing defensively, thinking, *I have to get him before he gets me.* In her mind it's going to be the "survival of the fittest," and she must win. If you choose to do battle with your children on any level, you will loose. The only answer is to respond in love, knowledge, and awareness.

A child whose temperament is different from his parents and the other children can be easily misunderstood as well. At this stage you might think that it takes a lot to be a parent, and you are right. If we don't become aware of our children's temperaments, we might just give up on some of them. I think of a young man who was never understood by his parents. He was defiant and irritable; his parents and their two other children were sensitive and compliant. When I first met him at fifteen, his parents had pitched him out of the house. They had decided that he was not going to stay at home and "corrupt" the other children. They had never taken the time and energy to understand and love him according to his bent.

The degree to which children meet up to parental expectations can also affect the relationship. We all want to claim as our own the young man who hits the home run, but we sometimes neglect the one who strikes out. We all want the A student, but will we as readily accept the D student?

Good Parents, Bad Kids

Perhaps we can learn from the father of the prodigal son. In Luke 15:20, when the son was returning to the father, it states, "But when he was yet a great way off, his father saw him, and had compassion, and ran, and fell on his neck, and kissed him." I wonder how many of us would have that attitude toward one of our youngsters who had squandered away half our wealth.

But if the father in the prodigal son parable was so great, how come his kids were so bad? I would be in anguish thinking that my son was sleeping with a prostitute. I'm not sure that I would give my son his inheritance if I thought he would squander it in "riotous living." Some parents are fortunate and foreordained to have the right balance between their children's temperaments and the environment created by their own temperaments. Others, such as the father mentioned in Luke 15, can be just as spiritual and just as concerned and still have difficult children. Proverbs 22:6 is an ideal toward which to reach. Many good parents have problem children.

If we have tried our best as parents, and our children have nevertheless turned out bad, the tendency is to feel guilty. *Where did we go wrong?* we ask. Realize that carrying excessive guilt accomplishes nothing. Paul gave us a good guideline in Philippians 3:13, when he wrote, "Forgetting those things which are behind, I press toward the mark of the prize of the high calling in Christ Jesus." "Forgetting those things which are behind" means not dwelling on the past and realizing that every day is a new beginning.

Because we can leave the past behind and press onward, we need not keep on making the same mistakes in the present. I'd like to simplify studies done on environmental considerations by Chess, Birch, and Thomas and to present briefly some environmental mistakes that parents can make.

Stretching

Sometimes parents stretch the child beyond his capacity. Our expectations are greater than the child's abilities. An insecure perfectionist parent may want to reproduce himself in the child, and he may destroy the child as he tries to squeeze him into an impossible mold. As Christians, we may hold up an image of the perfect Christian for our children to live up to. But the child himself should be the starting point. First we need to understand his abilities, his temperament, and his potential, and then we move him at his pace, not ours.

Stresses

There are stresses placed on the child outside the home. Frequently what is expected from the child at home doesn't mesh with what is expected from him at school and among his friends. Often the best Christian kids have to work to find suitable friends in their schools. The devil and the world apply a great deal of pressure on our children. Many years ago I heard Howard Hendricks from Dallas Theological Seminary explain that if you take the average amount of time that the best Christian spends in church compared to the time he spends in front of his television set, you find that by the time he is 65, he will have spent 9 months of his life in church and 16 years of his life in front of the TV. Parents must work hard to surround their youngsters with excellence. They need to find a church where there can be good fellowship and help for each of their children.

Shuffling

In constant mobility—shuffling from place to place—we can sacrifice both our own and our children's individuality. If career pressure leads us to move frequently, we should ask ourselves, "Are we driving our jobs, or are our jobs driving us?" It is easy for us to lose the picture of our children's needs when the compulsion of success continues to drive us.

Struggles

Struggles between the parents can affect the environment they create for their children. As parents struggle with each other, they model patterns of aggression for their children. Parents are a prime source of learning social behavior because their children see them as being powerful. Unfortunately, children model not only their parents' good social behavior but also their inappropriate behavior. Aggressive parents teach their children to behave aggressively as a dominant mode of dealing with daily frustrations.

In parental struggles there are basically three patterns. There are aggression patterns in which feelings are acted out; avoidance patterns, in which feelings are kept inside; and resolve patterns, in which feelings are worked through. You are modeling one of these behavior patterns for your child, and your behavior has far-reaching effects.

Shaping

Inconsistency in the shaping of the child by the parents adds stress to the child's environment. We should "walk our talk," keeping what we do in line with what we say. Can you imagine the confusion in the child if we tell him not to cheat on a test, and then he sees us cheating on our income taxes? Can you imagine the confusion if we are religious at church but heathen at home or if we pray at church but not at home? I recently spoke with a pastor who has divorced his wife and is living with another woman. I had previously counseled his daughter, who was having some difficulties. He is having a hard time realizing that his own infidelity and harsh treatment of the girl's mother could be a contributing factor in the girl's problem. We must work hard to "walk our talk."

Security

If the security needs of the child are not being met, this can create perhaps the harshest of the stresses on the child's environment. All of us need love and affection. Insecure parents who are searching for ways to control their children may hold back these ingredients, thinking that molding the children is more important than meeting emotional needs. What they don't understand is that meeting those emotional needs is a vital part of that molding process. In addition, as we meet our children's emotional needs, our own needs are met.

All home environments either create or relieve pressure. Teenagers either enjoy being at home with their parents or hate it. The home is either an oasis or a desert.

I recall a young woman relating her rationale in marrying at sixteen. "My father was an alcoholic," she said, "and on this particular Thanksgiving Day my mother had worked hard to fix dinner. My father left early in the morning for the bar, and when he arrived home at dinnertime, he was not only drunk he was angry. He proceeded to pull the tablecloth off the table, and while the dinner was on the floor, he grabbed my mother by the back of the neck and made her eat off the floor."

The she continued, "How much of that could you take before you would be looking for a way to escape?"

That's a hard question to answer.

This chart will give to you an opportunity to measure the degree of pressure placed on your children.

CUTHBERTSON CHILD STRESS INVENTORY

The purpose of this inventory is to measure the pressure that parents place on their children. Children vary in their responses to pressure and its effect on them. Pressure can lead to motivation and high performance, or it can lead to frustration and ineptness, depending on the makeup of the individual child.

For each factor choose a number from one to ten to represent the degree of stress you feel you put on your children. Add up the numbers and place the total at the bottom. Compare your total score with the chart for correlation.

FACTOR	DEFINITION AND SCALE	YOUR SCALE
STRETCHING push child little	*your expectations of the child* *1---------------5---------------10*	_____ push child much
STRESSES little social pressure	*pressures on child outside home* *1---------------5---------------10*	_____ much social pressure
SHUFFLING move little	*mobility, how much moving* *1---------------5---------------10*	_____ move much
STRUGGLES little home tension	*conflict between parents* *1-----------5-----------10*	_____ much home tension
SHAPING consistent example	*consistency of your lifestyle* *1---------------5---------------10*	_____ inconsistent example
SECURITY much love & affection	*meeting emotional needs of child* *1---------------5---------------10*	_____ little love & affection
		TOTAL _____

CHART CORRELATION
44–60—unreasonable stress and motivation on child
30–43—above average stress and motivation on child

18-29—average stress and motivation on child
 0-17—motivation needed on child

Patterns of Discipline

One notable study of parental discipline was done by W.C. Becker from the University of Illinois. He titled his findings, "Consequences of Parental Discipline." The essay is located in *Review of Child Development Research*, edited by Martin and Lois Hoffman.

Becker's study ties together numerous studies on parent behavior and discipline, and the results of his work suggest that it may be important to consider at least three general dimensions of parent behavior: warmth vs. hostility; restrictiveness vs. permissiveness; and anxious-emotional vs. calm-detachment.

> The *warmth* versus hostility dimension is defined at the warm end by variables of the following sort: accepting, affectionate, approving, understanding, child-centered, frequent use of explanations, positive response to dependency behavior, high use of reasons in discipline, high use of praise in discipline, low use of physical punishment, and (for mothers) low criticism of husband. The *hostility* end of the dimension would be defined by the opposite characteristics. The *restrictiveness* versus permissiveness dimension is defined at the restrictive end by: many restrictions and strict enforcement of demands in the areas of sex play, modesty behavior, table manners, toilet training, neatness, orderliness, care of household furniture, noise, obedience, aggression to siblings, aggression to peers, and aggression to parents.[10]

Permissiveness, obviously, would be the opposite of these. Becker describes anxious emotional involvement as being characterized by strong emotions regarding the child and "babying, protectiveness, and solicitousness for the child's welfare."[11]

Each of our homes falls into one of three general patterns of discipline: (1) authoritarian, (2) democratic, or (3) laissez-faire. Drawing from studies by Dusek, Meyer breaks this down more extensively.[12]

TYPE	DESCRIPTION
Autocratic	Parent tells the adolescent just what to do and allows little initiative or assertiveness.
Authoritarian	Parent tells the adolescent what to do but listens to adolescent's point of view.
Democratic	Parent allows ample opportunity for adolescents to make their own decisions but retains final authority.
Equalitarian	Parents and adolescents are involved equally in making decisions about the adolescent's behavior.
Permissive	Adolescent makes his own decisions, but parents like to be heard and have input.
Laissez-faire	Adolescent makes his own decisions and need not listen to the parent.
Ignoring	Adolescent makes his own decisions, and the parents don't care what the decisions are.

It is hoped that your own pattern is becoming more apparent. Becker notes that parents of different temperaments tend to fall into different discipline patterns.

Both the democratic parent and the indulgent parent are high on the dimensions of warmth and permissiveness, but the indulgent parent is high on emotional involvement while the democratic parent tends to be low on this dimension. Both the organized-effective parent and the overprotective parent are high on warmth and restrictiveness, but the overprotective parent again shows more emotional involvement than the organized-effective parent."[13]

Which Is Better?

Consistent with Becker's study, all homes could be categorized as warm-restrictive, warm-permissive, permissive-hostile, or restrictive-hostile. What is your own home like? Parents who have established restrictive-hostile or even warm-restrictive homes are apt to be stronger willed than those who have established more permissive atmospheres. This will effect the parenting mode. On the other hand, parents who have established a warm-permissive home might not see the need for the will modification process.

Obviously, the conclusion would be that the warm-permissive or the warm-restrictive homes are better and healthier for the child. Parents should work to have a loving, warm home. The key variable is the permissive-restrictive factor. In any case it is imperative not only that the parents are in control, but that they are working toward the proper will modification of the youngster.

The following inventory will help you discern which of the four patterns (warm-permissive, warm-restrictive, permissive-hostile or hostile-restrictive) characterizes your home. The inventory is followed by some guidelines for how to handle children of different temperaments in each of the environment types.

CUTHBERTSON ENVIRONMENT INVENTORY

The purpose of this inventory is to help you better understand your home environment. We as parents establish this environment, and each of our children responds differently to it. After you have determined into which category your home fits, you can match each of your children's temperaments to that environment and better plan your role as a parent.

For each of the twenty items on the inventory, rank the response options from 1–4, with 4 corresponding to what would be most typical for your home, and 1 corresponding to what would be least typical. You might also ask your children to complete the inventory, as they can sometimes help us see more clearly those areas about which we might have blind spots.

1. If your child talked back to you, to what extent would you be apt to do each of the following?

    _____ A. Dismiss him from your presence with minimal response.

    _____ B. Send him to his room and talk with him later.

    _____ C. Immediately spank him.

    _____ D. Respond verbally and inwardly figure this is part of his growing up.

2. To what extent does each of the following correspond to your approach to discipline?

    _____ A. Laissez-faire with little physical contact—my role is to create an atmosphere for the child's development.

    _____ B. Constructive guilt—I try to stop the bad behavior by helping the child realize he is responsible to others and to me.

    _____ C. Corporal punishment—the child's will must be modified if his spirit is to be saved.

    _____ D. Respected individuality—I want to respect his rights to individual opinions.

3. When I was growing up, to be spanked by my father:

    _____ A. would be unheard of; he believed corporal punishment should not be used.

    _____ B. happened very seldom, and the few times it did I felt I deserved it; he seemed apologetic about it.

    _____ C. happened many times and was probably a factor in making me very strong willed.

    _____ D. happened seldom, but when it did my father would be in a real rage.

4. Which sentence best describes communication in your home?
   _____ A. I wish I could get my spouse to talk more; I have a difficult time knowing what he or she is thinking.
   _____ B. There is much criticism; I wish we could have a more positive atmosphere in our home.
   _____ C. There are many arguments; it seems no matter what we discuss, it ends up in an argument.
   _____ D. Everyone seems to live in his or her own world; it seems as if there is little mutual concern.

5. Which sentence best describes your family's social life?
   _____ A. We have many friends and we get along with all of them well.
   _____ B. Even though we have many friends, we have few close ones.
   _____ C. We seem to lose friends very easily.
   _____ D. We have a few select friends.

6. As your children were growing up, which sentence best describes their relationships with their siblings and friends?
   _____ A. They seemed to become independent early in their lives.
   _____ B. They learned to depend on one another and mutually support one another as needed.
   _____ C. There was much confrontation; they argued a lot.
   _____ D. They lived in different worlds; they went their separate ways.

7. Which sentence best describes your family structure?
   _____ A. Loose structure—we do many things as a family, but we are all quite independent.
   _____ B. Close structure—we do many things as a family and we have learned to depend on one another.
   _____ C. Tight structure—we do few things as a family, and it seems as if we can never please one another.
   _____ D. Free structure—we do few things as a family, and we all live pretty much in our own worlds.

8. Which statement best describes your home?
   _____ A. There is little criticism between husband and wife.

_____ B. We expect our children to be submissive to us as parents.

_____ C. There is freedom for us to be ourselves.

_____ D. There seems to be little concern for others' needs.

9. If you were eating in a restaurant, which would best describe your expectations of your children?

_____ A. I would expect my children to be well groomed and sociable.

_____ B. I would expect my children to be polite and obedient.

_____ C. I would expect my children to be quiet and to mind me.

_____ D. I would expect my children to be themselves but to be respectful.

10. To what extent does each of the following correspond to your views on your children's clothing?

_____ A. We expect them to be clean and orderly.

_____ B. We expect them to be conservative in their dress.

_____ C. We understand that they need to be style conscious because they don't want to feel out of place in their peer groups.

_____ D. We want them to be clean, but we let them wear what is comfortable to them.

11. In our home, I have learned to be:

_____ A. very independent and make decisions by myself.

_____ B. dependent on other family members.

_____ C. able to fight for my rights and not to let anyone push me around.

_____ D. very dependent and lean heavily on others for support.

12. Which statement best describes your feelings on your child's future?

_____ A. We have high expectations; we live in a very competitive world.

_____ B. We feel our role is to help our child find his place in society.

_____ C. We expect him to work hard to find his place in life.

_____ D. We feel he knows what this society is like; what he does is up to him.

13. To what extent does each of the following describe your home?

_____ A. We have few rules for our children to follow; we want them to have the freedom to express themselves.

_____ B. We do not have rules but our kids know that there is a certain pattern of conduct expected of them.

_____ C. We have definite rules for our children to follow, and they know that they have to adhere to them.

_____ D. We realize that we had too many rules when we were growing up, but our children know what is expected of them.

14. Which sentence best describes your home?

_____ A. We have an adequate emotional atmosphere at home; affection is expressed.

_____ B. We are a very affectionate family; sometimes affection is used for reward or to create guilt.

_____ C. We have some affection in our family, but we argue a lot.

_____ D. We do not show much affection.

15. How do you feel about your child's future?

_____ A. He might as well realize early that it's a hard world out there.

_____ B. He will be thrown into reality quickly enough; I hope we can be a buffer to help him just a bit.

_____ C. Today's youth need to listen more to adults to understand how life really is.

_____ D. It might be a hard education, but society is a good place for them to learn.

16. If my spouse caught our children stealing from us, he or she would:

_____ A. do little the first time, but would be more harsh if it happened again.

_____ B. have them apologize and probably punish them.

_____ C. spank them.

_____ D. feel a certain sense of failure as a parent and react strongly.

17. If our child came across our clean floor with muddy shoes, we would most likely:

_____ A. have him clean up his mess and not punish him.

_____ B. be upset and probably punish him.

_____ C. spank him.

_____ D. be very upset that we are going to have to both punish him and clean the floor again.

18. When administering punishment, I usually:

_____ A. make the child feel guilty.

_____ B. talk first and act later—I would probably find out why
the action happened and only administer punishment
if needed.

_____ C. act first and talk later—I would probably spank and
send him to his room and talk with the child about why
the action was wrong.

_____ D. administer punishment in accord with the offense—
minor things warrant little punishment, major things
warrant more severe punishment.

19. Which statement best describes your relationship to your children?

_____ A. Our communication is not very good.

_____ B. They are too dependent on me.

_____ C. We seem to be distant, and we argue too much.

_____ D. It seems as if our wills clash quite often.

20. As a parent, I feel that my role is to:

_____ A. create an atmosphere where my children can find
themselves.

_____ B. help my children discover their abilities.

_____ C. direct my children away from evil factors in our
society.

_____ D. be there if needed but certainly not smother my
children.

Scoring

Each response option (A, B, C, and D) corresponds to one of the four
environment types. Descriptions of these follow. The four categories[14]
with respective definitions are:

A—*Warm-permissive:* The expectations on the children are high.
Children are expected to be neat. There is little criticism. The parents are socially outgoing. There is little rule enforcement of

children. Children are given a great amount of freedom. Children assume adult roles early and many times easily. There are few incidents of aggression. Parents have a tendency to flee rather than fight if there are problems. There is a good deal of independent communication between parents and children.

The major characteristics are *FREEDOM* and *INDEPENDENCE*.

B—*Warm-restrictive:* The children in this home are expected to be obedient. The home is characterized by a strong environment of love and affection. Physical affection is needed and encouraged. Parents and children generally act out their feelings. Family members tend to be dependent. The parents feel that their role is to protect their children. Often the children are withdrawn, depending on the strength of the parents. There is generally a minimum amount of aggression, again depending on the strength of the wills and personalities of the parents. Many times family members are mistrustful of people and therefore stay within their own family structure. The children are expected to be dependent on the adults. Sometimes it is difficult for the children to become independent and find their own freedom. There is a great self-imposed demand for perfection.

The major characteristics are *OBEDIENCE* and *DEPENDENCE*.

C—*Restrictive-hostile:* There is an exceptional amount of acting out of feelings. The home is characterized by excessive arguing, which leads to verbal and sometimes physical abuse. This leads to conflict among siblings. The children tend either to become very outspoken about their feelings or to withdraw rather than compete. Therefore, the behavior of children from these homes tends toward extremes, aggressive or shy, depending on the temperament of the child. A self-imposed demand for perfection can lead to strong competitive or dominating behavior. Parents often punish themselves through abuse, and the children frequently have a hard time growing up emotionally. The parents come down hard on the children's behavior. Spanking is usually used in excess.

The major characteristics are *DOMINANCE* and *AGGRESSION*.

D—*Permissive-hostile:* The parents tend to feel inadequate in their knowledge of raising children. Often they take on an attitude of indifference toward the child. The child is allowed a great deal of freedom. Many times the psychological and emotional needs of the child are neglected. The children have difficulty finding adult models to follow; they lean on their friends more. The children can develop very strong tendencies toward feelings of inadequacy and insecurity. The parents place other priorities above their children, and so there are poor parent-child relationships. Parents meet problems with physical discipline. Parents are inconsistent in their discipline.

The major characteristics are *INDIFFERENCE* and *INADEQUACY*.

Add up your numbered responses (1–4) for each environment type (A, B, C, and D). The highest score represents the most decisive environmental quality in your home.

The Environment and the Temperament
In chapter 9 you determined the temperaments of each of your children. You have also determined the type of home environment that you have established. Now is the time to put these two decisive factors together: how can I best raise my child in this environment? In this section you will find some brief guidelines for the molding of the child's will, the modeling by the parents, and the method of training used by the parents.

The Defiant Child

If your home environment is *warm-permissive:*

MOLD the will slowly. Develop patience through the impulsiveness and outbursts. Don't overlook psychological and emotional needs of the child. Work hard to see his individuality. Keep track of the child's progress.

MODEL—Recognize the difference in personalities. Work to be a friend, not a disciplinarian.

METHOD—Keep the child involved and work to channel the energy into constructive areas. Establish firm rules, and review the consequences *before* a possible incident, not after it has happened.

If your home environment is *warm-restrictive:*

MOLD the will slowly. Be careful about strong submission expectation. You need to drive him to warmth, rather than letting him drive you to hostility. Chart changes in the child's behavior.

MODEL—Be careful of will vs. will confrontation. Recognize that he needs love, affection, and belonging; change him through meeting those needs.

METHOD—Be careful of excessive corporal punishment. Strong wills could be developed, and the meaning of discipline lost if there is too much discipline.

If your home is *restrictive-hostile:*

MOLD the will carefully. This combination can be destructive. The strength of your wills could clash with his temperament. Be objective and keep track of progress.

MODEL—Learn to speak softly (Proverbs 15:1). Avoid confrontations, as they can be very destructive. He needs your example and a relationship with you.

METHOD—Avoid excessive corporal punishment. Spend much time with him and be loving.

If your home environment is *permissive-hostile:*

MOLD the will systematically. Purpose to make the child number one on your time and priority schedule. Work on patience and chart changes.

MODEL—Learn to speak softly (Proverbs 15:1). Avoid confrontation. Give to him much love and affection.

METHOD—Avoid excessive corporal punishment. Isolate the child and work hard to meet his psychological and emotional needs.

The Irritable Child

If your home environment is *warm-permissive:*

MOLD the will purposefully. The quickness and impulsiveness of the child will need guidance. You must take an active interest. Take one facet of the personality and chart the progress.

MODEL—Your example must be consistent. This child will be sensitive to flaws more than others.

METHOD—Spend time with the child. You must have much patience and love. They will need rule establishment and reinforcement from you.

If your home environment is *warm-restrictive:*

MOLD the will carefully. The impulsiveness of the child's personality and the restrictiveness of the parents could come into conflict. You must determine the child's potential. Chart progress.

MODEL—Lean on the warmth in your environment. They will be most responsive to a strong love approach.

METHOD—Be careful of will vs. will confrontation. The child will respond well to love and love withdrawal approach.

If your home environment is *restrictive-hostile:*

MOLD the will lovingly. Be careful not to break the spirit with the will. This could be very destructive with strong wills. Chart a course.

MODEL—You must work to be a loving example. Speak softly (Proverbs 15:1). Walk away from arguments.

METHOD—Avoid excessive corporal punishment as much

as possible. Spend much time with the child. Practice love and communication.

If your home environment is *permissive-hostile:*

MOLD the will systematically. As above you must be careful not to break the spirit with the will. The child must sense that he is important to you. Chart the course and avoid will vs. will confrontation.

MODEL—Work to be a loving example. Speak softly (Proverbs 15:1). Walk away from conflict.

METHOD—Avoid excessive corporal punishment as much as possible. Spend much time with the child. Practice love and communication.

The Sensitive Child

If your home environment is *warm-permissive:*

MOLD the will purposefully. The child will need encouragement and support. Meet dependency needs as you can. Don't misinterpret sensitivity as defiance.

MODEL—The child has strong security and love needs that must be met for the potential of the child to blossom. You can become the most important person in this child's life.

METHOD—There must be constant communication and affection. Love and love withdrawal can be very effective, but don't lean too heavily on the guilt.

If your home environment is *warm-restrictive:*

MOLD the child carefully. The restrictiveness and sensitivity can function well here if not overdone. The dependency needs will respond to rules.

MODEL—For the above to function well, the affection, love, and belonging needs must be met. Be careful not to make it difficult for the child to become independent.

METHOD—Avoid strong power assertion. They will respond to love withdrawal if not overdone.

If your home environment is *restrictive-hostile:*

MOLD the child carefully. This combination can be devastating. If you are not careful, you will break the spirit of the child. That could be irrevocable.

MODEL—Become sensitive to the child's need for affection, love, and belonging. Don't overpower the child with your personality.

METHOD—The child will respond well to love withdrawal, if not overdone. Strong power assertion could drive the child into shyness or withdrawal.

If your home environment is *permissive-hostile:*

MOLD the child systematically. This child needs your support; therefore, you must meet the child's needs, especially the needs of security and dependency.

MODEL—This child wants you to be his model. Don't let him down. Be patient with the child and realize that you can be a good and effective parent.

METHOD—Avoid strong power assertion. The child will respond well to love withdrawal if not overdone.

The Compliant Child

If your home environment is *warm-permissive:*

MOLD the will decisively. There might be a tendency to take the child for granted and not meet his needs. Stimulate curiosity and creativity within him.

MODEL—Your personalities could be very compatible. Foster a close relationship, work hard on communication, see him as a person, and meet his psychological and emotional needs.

METHOD—He will respond well to love and love withdrawal if used correctly. Spend time with him.

If your home environment is *warm-restrictive:*

MOLD the will decisively. You don't want to squelch abilities and creativity. Don't bear down too hard on the child. He will respond well to love.

MODEL—Don't smother the child. This child will grow best from the *warm* rather than the restrictive part of your personality You can have a wonderful relationship with this child.

METHOD—He will respond well to love and love withdrawal if used correctly. Work hard to have good communication with the child.

If your home environment is *restrictive-hostile:*

MOLD the will purposefully. There will be a danger here of breaking the spirit with the will. Don't bear down too hard on the child. If he turns on you with his temperament, it could be irrevocable.

MODEL—Work to soften your personality and not be defensive. This youngster needs love and communication and he can be a real joy to you.

METHOD—He will respond best to love and love withdrawal. Avoid excessive corporal punishment.

If your home environment is *permissive-hostile:*

MOLD the will carefully. It might be easy here to gravitate to separate worlds and consequently not meet the child's needs.

MODEL—Be sure that discipline and love are balanced. The child will look to you to meet his needs—don't disappoint him.

METHOD—He will respond best to love and love withdrawal. Avoid will vs. will confrontation and excessive corporal punishment. You don't want to turn this gem into a rock.

"Modify the will of the child in accord with the bent": discipline is the means by which this goal is reached. Assertive Scriptural Parenting demands that you have the right attitude and the right skills to produce the right product. And remember-anything worth attaining demands work.

11

Not a Hearer Only

These last two chapters are the most important in the book. Thus far, we have tried to appeal to your mind with the goal of imparting knowledge; now we want to appeal to your spirit with the goal of imparting understanding. You see, perception is everything. There are at least four levels of parenting mentality: (1) those that have the wrong knowledge and reinforce it; (2) those that have some right knowledge, but don't apply it; (3) those that lack knowledge, realize it, but don't go after it; and (4) those that have understanding. The by-products of these mentalities could be illustrated by their response, let's say, to a Bible study seminar. For those in the first group, the material either goes over their heads or it conflicts with what they have already concluded, so they don't change. Those who fall into the second category become very excited over what they have learned and for a few weeks they are different; but little by little they fall back into their old ways. Those in the third group religiously follow every "jot and tittle" of the teaching they have heard, but without thinking the ideas through for themselves. People who fall into the fourth group see a bigger picture. It is not merely the teachings that excite them, but also the new way of thinking. They begin to get into the Word themselves and to make personal application of the Scriptures to their lives.

Note the parallels between these four groups and the four types of soil in the Parable of the Sower in Luke 8:4-8. In this passage the seed is sown on four different types of soil. The seed that fell by the wayside was immediately "trodden down" or devoured by birds. The seed that fell on the rocky soil withered away for lack of moisture as soon as it began to spring up. The seed that fell among the thorns was eventually choked by them. But the seed that fell on good ground sprang up and bore fruit in abundance. In the same way each of you will respond differently to what you are reading. Some of you will change and your homes will be different; some of you will not.

Steps to Understanding

In counseling we take the patient through three different levels: realization, restructuring, and reinforcement. I contend that a person can't move toward righteousness unless he realizes his "wrongeousness." Once a person realizes where he has gone wrong, he must be willing to change and rebuild, and finally a new pattern can develop.

This chapter will deal with *realization*. Note that in the Parable of the Sower the seed in three of the four types of soil began to grow, but only the seed that fell on good ground flourished. Only in the good soil was a new pattern established. This illustrates the need not only for realization but also for restructuring, which will be discussed in the next chapter, along with reinforcement.

Our goal in realization is to experience understanding. Theologically, it might be called "illumination." Psychologically, it might be called "self-realization." Basically, the thought is, "I see it differently now. I am willing to change. I never realized that before."

After the Resurrection Jesus appeared to two disciples on the road to Emmaus, as recorded in Luke 24. The word *open* appears in this passage three times. First, Jesus *opened* the Scriptures (vv. 27, 32). Then He *opened* their eyes (v. 31). And then finally in verse 45 He "*opened* their understanding."

I am intrigued both by the progression and by the experience. It seems that if I don't open the Scriptures, then my eyes will not be opened. And if I want to experience understanding, then I first need to have my eyes opened. But what difference does understanding make in my life? And how do I get there?

In the Book of Proverbs the experience of understanding is the ultimate goal. Proverbs 3:13-15 speaks of its value. "Happy is the man that findeth wisdom, and the man that getteth understanding. For the merchandise of it is better than the merchandise of silver, and the gain thereof than fine gold. She is more precious than rubies; and all the things thou canst desire are not to be compared unto her." The Book of Proverbs also speaks of the by-products of understanding: it gives us access to wisdom (14:33), it enables us to be "slow to wrath" (14:29), and it enables us to have an "excellent spirit" (17:27).

Proverbs 15:32 even tells me how to get it: "He that refuseth instruction despiseth his own soul, but he that heareth reproof getteth understanding." My response toward rebuke becomes the catalyst for change. It becomes the key that unlocks the door to understanding. Proverbs 24:3 states that "through wisdom is an house builded, and by understanding it is established." Many individuals get their house started but never get it finished.

Philippians 4:6-7 gives to us the ultimate goal of understanding. "Be anxious for nothing; but in everything, by prayer and supplication with thanksgiving, let your requests be made known unto God. And the peace of God, which passeth all understanding, shall keep your hearts and minds through Christ Jesus." How would you like to experience understanding? How would you like to have a peace that passeth understanding?

How Can I Begin?

Through the material given thus far, you can realize that God desires to modify your will. You can realize that your kids have a decisive old nature, and that the will of your child must be modified. You can realize that you must constantly ask yourself the question "What am I observing?" with regard to your children. You can realize that God has placed a particular bent within each of your children, that there are different types of bents, and that the will must be modified in accord with the child's bent. You can realize that your home environment will have an effect on this process.

Patterns for Life

You can realize as well that the outcome of each of your children is predictable. (Stop for a moment and let *that* sink in!) Remember that Proverbs 22:6 can be understood as meaning that we are to modify the will of the child in accord with the bent placed in the child by God, and that if we do that successfully, the pattern developed will be lifelong. That means that if the bent is understood and the will modified accordingly, then the pattern can be predictable and each child can be reared as an individual.

What pattern am I observing? Certainly, each of the various predispositions mentioned in chapter 9 will evolve into a pattern. These patterns of childhood continue in large measure into adult life.

Observing the pattern is a first step, but any of the factors mentioned in chapter 9 can be properly or improperly reinforced. Take for instance the mood of the child. Now that I am knowledgeable about the mood of my child, how do I respond? I can mellow it and develop it, or I can beat it into the ground and not allow it to be expressed. What is good in the pattern must be encouraged; what is bad should be discouraged.

By taking time to become knowledgeable of each of my children's predispositions, I can anticipate possible future patterns. Knowledge is power and understanding is dynamite. You can predict the outcome of each of your children.

Hope for Every Child

You can realize that each of your children can potentially be reached. Let's explore this from a spiritual perspective.

The Scriptures relate in Genesis 1:27 that we were created in the image of God. It is interesting to correlate the concepts of "the image of God" and one's "conscience." All of us have within us the ability to discern right and wrong and good and bad. But what is the source of this ability? And what are its ramifications?

Let's tackle these questions. If God has a potentially perfect plan for every person before he is born (Ps. 139:13-16, 2 Tim. 1:9), it would seem logical that He would establish a potential for goodness within every child. In order for the child to respond to goodness that potential would have to be there. Our conscience bears witness of God. We have a "God consciousness." We have His imprintation on us. The capacity for guilt and the capacity to discern right and wrong stems from God's "image," in which we are made. As long as the conscience is not "seared" (1 Tim. 4:2), it can be used by the Holy Spirit to convict us of our sin, to lead us to acknowledge our sin nature, and to bring us to God through Jesus Christ.

The image of God *did* in part survive the Fall; therefore, potentially every child can be reached. Let me reiterate that: every child can be reached. You may protest that your child is beyond hope, but I say that the only problem with your child is that he was born into what appears to be the wrong family. Now before you throw this book hastily into the wastebasket, let me defend my statement. If your child had been born to parents of different temperaments, would he still have the same experiences and problems? If you had responded differently to your child than you have, would your child have grown up the same way? All of this is conjecture, of course;

others might have made mistakes where you succeeded. Even though the interaction of your temperaments as parents with the child's temperament may not make it easy, because of God's image in him, that child can be reached.

But What about the Fall?

Genesis 1:26-27 gives us the characteristics of the image of God in man before the Fall: "And God said, 'Let us make man in Our image, after Our likeness; and let them have dominion over the fish of the sea, and over the fowl of the air, and over the cattle, and over all the earth, and over every creeping thing that creepeth upon the earth.' So God created man in His own image, in the image of God created He him; male and female created He them." From this passage we can conclude that (1) man was a rational creature, with the ability to make intelligent decisions, and to store and pass on knowledge; (2) man had volition and conscience, with the choice of following or rejecting God's commands; and (3) man was created without sin. After man was created God stated that it was good (1:31).

After the Fall, however, the sin nature developed, but we retained our intellect and volition. In place of sinless innocence came guilt (Gen. 3:7-13). Therefore, you can constructively use three factors in raising a child after the Fall: (1) the intellect—you can teach and reason with him; (2) volition—you can recognize his ability to choose and encourage his hunger for spiritual things; and (3) guilt—you can help him see his sin nature so that he will be more responsive to truth.

The conscience is an essential part of the image of God in fallen man. Carl Henry writes that the conscience is "God's most intimate presence within the soul of man."[15] E.G. Robinson calls the conscience the "rational power of the soul by which all distinctions of whatever kind are perceived and judgments pronounced."[16]

There are four conclusions then to consider. The first is that *man is still the bearer of the image of God.* Carl Henry writes that the image of God "in fallen man is shattered but not destroyed."[17] The second conclusion is that *natural, unregenerate man retains an innate knowledge of good.* As Matthew 7:11 asserts, "If ye then, being evil, know how to give good gifts unto your children, how much more shall your Father which is in heaven give good things to them that ask Him?" Third, *the conscience has the capacity to acquit as well as condemn* (1 Cor. 4:4, 2 Cor. 1:12). Finally, *conscience is the moral agent in man.* "It speaks with dramatic right, addressing man with terrible earnestness as his proximate moral authority."[18]

There are men and women who are shining examples of God's mercy and grace. They were once on drugs, or they were alcoholics, or they were sexually promiscuous. But God took hold of their lives and changed them. What capacity did they have within them that enabled them to change? Even though they once seemed beyond hope, these people *did* change. No matter how hopeless it seems, change is always possible. This is true for your child as well.

Every child goes through an environmental grid, that is, depending on what our homes are like, how well we understand our youngsters' temperaments, how well we understand the sovereignty of God, and how well we understand the components of God's image (intellect, volition, guilt potential), that child's conscience will move through either positive or negative steps. In one case an initial step of goodness leads to a complete or whole conscience. In another case, an initial step toward an "evil" conscience can lead to a "searing" or deadening of the conscience. This is a real tragedy. I believe that anything short of "searing" can be reversed. God always wants reconciliation.

The conscience can be used to reach our children or to destroy them. The child can eventually decide that it is good to have daily family devotions, or the child, because of the wounding of the conscience, can decide that it is OK to be aggressive like his dad. He likes his dad, and his dad is aggressive. Therefore, he reasons, there must be nothing wrong with being aggressive. The conscience is part of the very fabric of human personality. It is essential to the image of God, and it can be exploited properly by godly parents to develop godly children. The perceptive parent draws from the child's innate knowledge of right and wrong, establishes a model to imitate, and then works hard to reinforce right conduct.

12

You Can Do It!

I once asked in the course of a conference, "If your children came to you and asked a spiritual question, would you have something to teach them?"

After the meeting a young engineer approached me. He said, "I've been a poor husband and father—I know little about the Bible. What should I do?"

I suggested he and his wife get some Christian literature and read it together and also that they take some courses together at a nearby Bible college.

The results were amazing. Together they became excited about the Word of God. They eventually left the area, attended a Christian college, and took on a pastorate on the West Coast.

This couple gives us an illustration of the pattern of realization, restructuring, and reinforcement. After they initially realized their need, they began to restructure their attitudes and activities, and that restructuring was subsequently reinforced. The end result was a great change in their lives. In the course of your reading so far, you may have come to a realization of a need to restructure your method of disciplining your children, to restructure your attitudes about discipline, to restructure your approach to a rebellious child, or to restructure your child rearing philosophy so as to rear each child according to his bent. What now?

Where Do I Go from Here?

Any time you decide to travel somewhere, you need to know where you are, where you're going, and how to get there. If you have realized where you want to go, in what ways you need to change in order to become a better parent, you need to be sure you know where you are right now. Perhaps surprisingly, it is very possible not to know where you are. Remember that in the Parable of the Sower, only some seed fell on the good ground. Other seed fell on rocky soil and thorny soil. At first it began to grow, but because of its environment, it died. Where it was made all the difference.

Do you really know where you are? Perhaps you're going on the assumption that your parents did it right, but maybe they didn't. Or perhaps you are not really ready to pay the price for change.

This is what Paul meant when he wrote in Philippians 4:8, "Finally, brethren, whatsoever things are true, whatsoever things are honest, whatsoever things are just, whatsoever things are pure, whatsoever things are lovely, whatsoever things are of good report; if there be any virtue, and if there be any praise, think on these things." We can take the kinds of positive things mentioned in this verse, think on them, practice them, and until finally they become part of us. This is what restructuring and reinforcement are all about. Psychologists call this "pattern therapy." It is not only good therapy; it is biblical. All of Scripture supports this psychological approach. You can only bring into parenting what you are. As the past has made the present, so the present will make the future. What you are is in part a result of experience upon experience stored within you. Your mind's storage area has various levels. Some experiences are close to the surface of your consciousness. Other experiences have been repressed and pushed deep into your memory. Often these are the ones that are most traumatic. It is these subconscious experiences that must be unlocked.

Our minds are somewhat like a bucket of dirty water after the car has been washed. The dirt from the car has been wrung out of the sponge into the water, just as our experiences have wrung out bad attitudes and ineffective coping patterns into our minds. The bucket of dirty water can simply be emptied and hosed out, but it is not that easy with our minds. The other choice with the bucket is to aim the running hose into the full bucket. As the clean water goes in, the dirty water comes out. This we can do with our minds.

You Can Get There!

I think most all of us would like to be better parents, but either we don't believe we can develop the right attitudes and skills or we aren't willing to pay the price to do so. But we can! Let me illustrate. I like to ask patients, "What should you do?" or "What shouldn't you be doing?" when they come to me with a problem. Interestingly, 99 out of 100 times they have the right solution. "Well, I really shouldn't be drinking" or "I really should spend more time with my family," they say. I didn't need to tell them what they should do. Through pattern psychology with reinforcement therapy not only can you move toward resolving many of your problems, but you can also have the fulfillment of personal involvement.

Let's try it. Jot down some conflict experiences you have had or are currently having. Then write down how you responded or are responding. How *should* you respond? If you need to change, set some practical goals for how you can respond in the future. Once you have derived a solution, then practice it; reinforce it until a new pattern is established.

Where Is God in All This?

God is a sovereign God; He is in control. He knows each of our individual situations, and He has a purpose in all that transpires. If "all things work together for good to them that love God" (Rom. 8:28), and if all things happen "after the counsel of His own will" (Eph. 1:11), and if God is striving to "will and to do of His good pleasure" in my life (Phil. 2:13), and if He is striving to finish that which He has begun in my life (1:6), then there are no such things as problems, just opportunities. God is active, and He has purpose and design in every situation in our lives as Christians. Proverbs 16:9 states that we direct our "way," but God directs our "steps."

Where you are right now is where God wants you to be. That is not to say that this is where you should remain, however. On the contrary, God is striving to modify our wills, and He can do this through situations where there is hurt and adversity. Proverbs 17:25 states that "A foolish son is a grief to his father, and bitterness to her that bare him." But we fathers and mothers can learn from that grief and bitterness. God can use even that to change us.

Attitudes, Skills, and Products

We need to start with the right attitudes as parents. When you face a potential conflict with your child, what goes through your mind? The right attitude means asking, "What am I observing?" not "What do I feel?" It is this that gets many of us into trouble. If I go from what I *feel,* I will be going downhill from the start.

When it comes to putting the proper skills to work, I need to ask the question, "How should I respond?" rather than, "What do I feel like doing?" We can't allow ourselves to be led by our emotions— the consequences in the life of the child are too important.

When it comes to the end result of the molding process, the products, the questions are, "What is my goal?" and "What patterns do I want to develop or change?" A laissez-faire approach—"what will be, will be"—will not result in the products we want.

Let's try it. You have just finished cleaning and waxing the kitchen floor, and as you walk into the living room your seven-year-old, irritable son starts across the kitchen floor with his muddy shoes on. What is your *attitude* in this situation? (Are you feeling or observing?) What *skills* do you apply? What is the *result?*

WRONG APPROACH
   Attitude: What do I feel?
   I feel rage; I am angry!
   Skill: What do I feel like doing?
   This kid is about to have the spanking of his life.
   Product: What happened?
   The child is overpunished; eventually he may become strong-willed.

RIGHT APPROACH
   Attitude: What is observed?
   Here is an impulsive child who is not thinking and who needs to be taught to be more responsible.
   Skill: What should I do?
   To reinforce responsibility, I will have him clean up the mess he made.
   Product: What is my goal?
   To cut into the pattern of impulsiveness and to teach him to become more responsible for his actions.

Let's try one more. Your two children get into an argument, and they come to blows. What do you think? What do you do?

WRONG APPROACH
   Attitude: What do I feel?
   Frustration and anger.
   Skill: What do I feel like doing?
   Beating them both up myself or letting them fight it out.
   Product: What happened?
   I am modeling for them how to deal with conflict situations improperly.

RIGHT APPROACH
Attitude: What is observed?
I have two children who don't know how to resolve their differences.
Skill: What should I do?
I will have them separate and talk it through, but they might need a cooling-off period first.
Product: What's my goal?
To teach them not to act out their feelings, but to resolve them.

You can see that you always have to be suspicious of what you feel at first. As patterns are developed both within you—in your teaching, training, and modeling—and within the children, then your spontaneous reactions will become more trustworthy. (Note that even through what must have been much pain, the father of the prodigal son was able to use the proper skills and solution—the door was left open for the boy to return home.) Of course skills must be reinforced. That boy will be back with his muddy shoes again. Those two children will probably fight again. But if you maintain the right attitude, apply the right skills, and keep your goals in mind, after a while, they will catch on, and new patterns will develop in them.

Our Lord's Example
Consider the challenge of Philippians 2:5: "Let this mind be in you, which was also in Christ Jesus." What were His attitudes, skills, and products like? Let's take a couple of examples.

In Mark 10:13-16 the people brought children to Jesus. Note the contrast between the disciples' approach to this situation and Jesus' approach.

And they brought young children to Him, that He should touch them: and His disciples rebuked those that brought them. But when Jesus saw it, He was much displeased, and said unto them,

'Suffer the little children to come unto Me, and forbid them not: for of such is the kingdom of God. Verily I say unto you, Whosoever shall not receive the kingdom of God as a little child, he shall not enter therein.' And He took them up in His arms, put His hands upon them, and blessed them.

WRONG APPROACH
Attitude: What is felt?
Disciples were upset; they rebuked the people.
Skill: What do they want to do?
They wanted to get both the adults and the children away from Jesus.
Product: What happened?
People's desire to come to Jesus would have been squelched.

RIGHT APPROACH
Attitude: What is observed?
Jesus sees people who need Him.
Skill: What does He do?
He takes them up into His arms.
Product: What is His goal?
He blesses them, building their self-worth.

The Bible is filled with similar scenes, in which the disciples or other people wanted one course of action and Jesus another. It is easy to see the contrasting attitudes, skills, and solutions. Another example is the woman taken in the act of adultery in John 8. The people were ready to stone her, but Jesus loved her. The people wanted to give her death, but Jesus wanted to give her life. The people wanted to punish, but Jesus wanted to teach.

Like Father, Like Son
We draw our modeling pattern from Jesus. Jesus' drew His from the Father. Scripture tells us of His attitude and skill: "whom the Lord loveth He chasteneth" (Heb. 12:6), and we also read of His goal:

"that we might be partakers of His holiness" (Heb. 12:10). The bottom line of biblical principle is always application. God desires to change us.

We too are aware that each of our children has a will that must be modified in accord with the bent God has placed in each child. We can see the products God desires to produce and we have confidence that our children can be reached, because God has created them in His image and given to them a conscience from which we can draw. We can establish patterns that we want to be reinforced, and we can work to be objective as we move toward those goals. We can decide that we are not going to let one of our children get away—not even one.

In his book *To Kiss the Joy,* Robert Raines relates the following incident:

A friend of mine was staying overnight in the home of a Yugoslav pastor and his wife and three boys sometime ago. Two of the boys were handsome, strong young men. They were going to the university and showing high promise. The third boy, twenty years old, was over in the corner of the room playing with his toys. My friend asked if he might take a picture of the family, thinking of the parents and the two normal boys, but the father said to him, "Wait a minute until I get him ready." The picture was taken with the retarded boy in the center. I learned something from that father about what it means to belong to the family. No child was missing from the picture, not one.

You and I belong to the Father's family, and not one of us is missing from that picture. Each of us at times feels ugly or unacceptable, but we are in the center of His family picture just as we are, loved by our Father. We are free to change and make changes, free to raise our children, not our voices.

Sic 'em, Fido!

Notes

1. Charles Swindoll, *You and Your Child* (Nashville: Thomas Nelson Publishers, 1977), p. 18.

2. Swindoll, *You and Your Child*, p. 19.

3. Bruce Narramore, *Help, I'm a Parent* (Grand Rapids, Michigan: Zondervan Publishers, 1971), pp. 37–44.

4. William J. Meyer and Jerome B. Dusek, *Child Psychology—A Developmental Perspective* (Lexington, Massachusetts: D.C. Heath and Company, 1979), p. 383.

5. Haim Ginott, *Between Parent and Child* (New York: Avon Publishers, 1956), p. 125.

6. Meyer and Dusek, *Child Psychology*, p. 382.

7. Alexander Thomas, Stella Chess, and Herbert Birch, *Temperament and Behavior Disorders in Children* (New York: New York University Press, 1968), p. 4.

8. Thomas, Chess, and Birch, *Temperament,* p. 191.

9. Thomas, Chess, and Birch, *Temperament,* p. 73.

10. W.C. Becker, "Consequences of Different Kinds of Parental Discipline," in M.L. Hoffman and L.W. Hoffman (Eds.), *Review of Developmental Research,* Vol. I (New York: Russell Sage Foundation, 1964), p. 174.

11. Becker, "Parental Discipline," p. 174.

12. Meyer and Dusek, *Child Psychology,* p. 538, adapted from Jerome B. Dusek, *Adolescent Development and Behavior* (Palo Alto, California: Science Research Associates, Inc., 1977).

13. Becker, "Parental Discipline," p. 174.

14. The four environmental categories are adapted from Becker, "Parental Discipline."

15. Carl F.H. Henry, *Christian Personal Ethics* (Grand Rapids, Michigan: Wm. B. Eerdmans Publishers, 1971), p. 517.

16. Ezekiel Robinson, *Principles and Practices of Morality* (Boston: Silver Burdett and Company, 1895), p. 29.

17. Henry, *Ethics,* p. 520.

18. Henry, *Ethics,* p. 519

More Victor Books for Your Family

How to Really Love Your Teenager
by Dr. Ross Campbell
Dr. Campbell provides practical ways to show your love and acceptance to your teens (6-2274). Also available is Dr. Campbell's *How to Really Love Your Child* (6-2751).

Parents and Teenagers
by Jay Kesler and Ronald A. Beers
A helpful reference book containing advice for parents of teenagers from over fifty Christian leaders, including Evelyn Christenson, Howard Hendricks, Charles Swindoll, and Warren Wiersbe (6-2817).

A Mother's Touch
by Elise Arndt
Guidelines for mothers of young children who desire to teach their little ones about God, values, life, and love (6-2101).

A Man's Touch
by Dr. Charles F. Stanley
A book for Christian husbands who want to be better leaders, lovers, providers, fathers, and teachers in their homes (6-2753).

Heaven Help the Home
by Howard G. Hendricks
Howard Hendricks' sound biblical advice will help you build a strong Christian home (6-2240).

How to Disciple Your Children
by Walter A. Henrichsen
A parent's most important job is discipling his own children. This book explores biblical principles for avoiding negative aspects of child rearing and discipling effectively (6-2260).